Applying Use Cases

The Addison-Wesley Object Technology Series

Grady Booch, Ivar Jacobson, and James Rumbaugh, Series Editors

For more information check out the series web site [http://www.awl.com /cseng/otseries/] as well as the pages on each book [http://www.awl.com/cseng/I-S-B-N/] (I-S-B-N represents the actual ISBN, including dashes).

David Bellin and Susan Suchman Simone, *The CRC Card Book*
ISBN 0-201-89535-8

Grady Booch, *Object Solutions: Managing the Object-Oriented Project*
ISBN 0-8053-0594-7

Grady Booch, *Object-Oriented Analysis and Design with Applications, Second Edition*
ISBN 0-8053-5340-2

Grady Booch, James Rumbaugh, and Ivar Jacobson, *The Unified Modeling Language User Guide*
ISBN 0-201-57168-4

Don Box, *Essential COM*
ISBN 0-201-63446-5

Don Box, Keith Brown, Tim Ewald, and Chris Sells, *Effective COM: 50 Ways to Improve Your COM and MTS-based Applications*
ISBN 0-201-37968-6

Alistair Cockburn, *Surviving Object-Oriented Projects: A Manager's Guide*
ISBN 0-201-49834-0

Dave Collins, *Designing Object-Oriented User Interfaces*
ISBN 0-8053-5350-X

Bruce Powel Douglass, *Real-Time UML: Developing Efficient Objects for Embedded Systems*
ISBN 0-201-32579-9

Desmond F. D'Souza and Alan Cameron Wills, *Objects, Components, and Frameworks with UML: The Catalysis Approach*
ISBN 0-201-31012-0

Martin Fowler, *Analysis Patterns: Reusable Object Models*
ISBN 0-201-89542-0

Martin Fowler with Kendall Scott, *UML Distilled: Applying the Standard Object Modeling Language*
ISBN 0-201-32563-2

Peter Heinckiens, *Building Scalable Database Applications: Object-Oriented Design, Architectures, and Implementations*
ISBN 0-201-31013-9

Ivar Jacobson, Grady Booch, and James Rumbaugh, *The Unified Software Development Process*
ISBN 0-201-57169-2

Ivar Jacobson, Magnus Christerson, Patrik Jonsson, and Gunnar Overgaard, *Object-Oriented Software Engineering: A Use Case Driven Approach*
ISBN 0-201-54435-0

Ivar Jacobson, Maria Ericsson, and Agneta Jacobson, *The Object Advantage: Business Process Reengineering with Object Technology*
ISBN 0-201-42289-1

Ivar Jacobson, Martin Griss, and Patrik Jonsson, *Software Reuse: Architecture, Process and Organization for Business Success*
ISBN 0-201-92476-5

David Jordan, *C++ Object Databases: Programming with the ODMG Standard*
ISBN 0-201-63488-0

Philippe Kruchten, *The Rational Unified Process: An Introduction*
ISBN 0-201-60459-0

Wilf LaLonde, *Discovering Smalltalk*
ISBN 0-8053-2720-7

Lockheed Martin Advanced Concepts Center and Rational Software Corporation, *Succeeding with the Booch and OMT Methods: A Practical Approach*
ISBN 0-8053-2279-5

Thomas Mowbray and William Ruh, *Inside CORBA: Distributed Object Standards and Applications*
ISBN 0-201-89540-4

Ira Pohl, *Object-Oriented Programming Using C++, Second Edition*
ISBN 0-201-89550-1

Rob Pooley and Perdita Stevens, *Using UML: Software Engineering with Objects and Components*
ISBN 0-201-36067-5

Terry Quatrani, *Visual Modeling with Rational Rose and UML*
ISBN 0-201-31016-3

Walker Royce, *Software Project Management: A Unified Framework*
ISBN 0-201-30958-0

James Rumbaugh, Ivar Jacobson, and Grady Booch, *The Unified Modeling Language Reference Manual*
ISBN 0-201-30998-X

Geri Schneider and Jason P. Winters, *Applying Use Cases: A Practical Guide*
ISBN 0-201-30981-5

Yen-Ping Shan and Ralph H. Earle, *Enterprise Computing with Objects: From Client/Server Environments to the Internet*
ISBN 0-201-32566-7

David N. Smith, *IBM Smalltalk: The Language*
ISBN 0-8053-0908-X

Daniel Tkach, Walter Fang, and Andrew So, *Visual Modeling Technique: Object Technology Using Visual Programming*
ISBN 0-8053-2574-3

Daniel Tkach and Richard Puttick, *Object Technology in Application Development, Second Edition*
ISBN 0-201-49833-2

Jos Warmer and Anneke Kleppe, *The Object Constraint Language: Precise Modeling with UML*
ISBN 0-201-37940-6

Applying Use Cases

A Practical Guide

Geri Schneider

Jason P. Winters

ADDISON-WESLEY

An imprint of Addison Wesley Longman, Inc.

Reading, Massachusetts • Harlow, England • Menlo Park, California
Berkeley, California • Don Mills, Ontario • Sydney
Bonn • Amsterdam • Tokyo • Mexico City

Many of the designations used by manufacturers and sellers to distinguish their products are claimed as trademarks. Where those designations appear in this book and Addison Wesley Longman Inc., was aware of a trademark claim, the designations have been printed in initial caps or all caps.

The authors and publisher have taken care in the preparation of this book, but make no expressed or implied warranty of any kind and assume no responsibility for errors or omissions. No liability is assumed for incidental or consequential damages in connection with or arising out of the use of the information or programs contained herein.

The publisher offers discounts on this book when ordered in quantity for special sales. For more information, please contact:

AWL Direct Sales
Addison Wesley Longman, Inc.
One Jacob Way
Reading, Massachusetts 01867

Library of Congress Cataloging-in-Publication Data

Schneider, Geri.
    Applying use cases : a practical guide / Geri Schneider, Jason P. Winters.
        p.   cm. — (Addison-Wesley object technology series)
    Includes bibliographical references and index.
    ISBN 0-201-30981-5 (alk. paper)
    1. Application software—Development.   2. Use cases (Systems engineering) I. Winters, Jason P.   II. Title.   III. Series.
QA76.76.A65S34   1998
005.3--dc21   98-29948
                                                              CIP

ISBN 0-201-30981-5

Visit AWL on the Web: www.awl.com/cseng/

Text printed on recycled and acid-free paper.

2 3 4 5 6 7   MA   01 00 99 98
2nd Printing December 1998

For Jason, my friend and my love.
He told me, "If you write it, I'll help."
And he did.

Contents

Foreword

When I first proposed a new set of modeling concepts back in 1967 as the result of my work on large telecommunication switching systems and system design, the idea of use cases as a method of analysis was very sketchy. With the emergence of object-oriented ideas and my subsequent work in applying OO in the 1980s and formalizing the principles underlying Objectory, use case analysis began to take better shape and to play a significant role in the analysis of the problem domain. Today the ideas embodied in use cases have matured, and this technique has become a significant tool that belongs in every analyst's toolkit.

With the incorporation of use cases into the industry standard modeling language, UML, it is time for a new book that illustrates the current notation and semantics of use cases in a practical, easy-to-understand manner. Use case analysis also plays a central role in the new Unified Process for software development. It is, therefore, critical that managers, architects, designers, analysts, domain experts, programmers, and testers understand how to apply use cases.

In *Applying Use Cases*, Geri Schneider and Jason Winters have done an excellent job of introducing this powerful technique and demonstrating its application in real-world settings. Rather than making everything perfect up front, the examples progress in much the same manner you would find in a real project, with early rough models being refined as the team gains understanding of the project. This realism allows the introduction of issues that would arise in actual projects. *Applying Use Cases* is easy to read, but contains a wealth of detail.

This book clearly reflects Geri's experience as a trainer for Rational Software, the time she has spent mentoring and training customers of Wyyzzk Training and Consulting, and the time Jason has spent using the techniques and mentoring engineers at Lucent Technologies. It is an excellent resource for anyone who needs to understand use case analysis, and I recommend it highly.

Ivar Jacobson

Preface

You're about to start a new project. Sometimes it seems like colonizing the moon would be easier. But you assemble a stalwart team and prepare to set sail on the good ship Requirements hoping to reach the fabled land of Success. They say there are no failed projects in Success and the profit margin is so high, the streets are paved with gold.

There are many dangers between here and Success. Many a ship is sunk on the way—some say as many as 80 percent never reach that fabled land. You query those who have tried before. "Use a ship from the OO line," they say. "Booch, OMT, OOSE, UML are all good models to choose from. You'll also need a chart showing risks along the way and an architecture of the major land masses. And finally you'll need to plot a course of use cases to reach your destination."

Use Cases are included in the Unified Modeling Language and are used throughout the Rational Unified Process. They are gaining wide acceptance in many different businesses and industries. Most often, use cases are applied to software projects and enterprise-wide applications.

This book is for anyone interested in applying use cases to project development. While we can't guarantee you will always have successful projects when using use cases, we can give you another way of looking at the projects you are developing and some tools that will make success more likely.

You will get more benefit out of the book if you have some basic knowledge of object-oriented concepts. We will use the Unified Modeling Language for the notation, explaining the notation as we use it. A good book to use for reference on the notation is *UML Distilled* by Fowler. This is an excellent book on the topic and easy to read.

This book is organized using the Rational Unified Process as a framework. Within the phases of the process, we talk about the activities in the phase, focusing on activities based on use cases. We touch lightly on activities that interact with use cases, such as software architecture, project management, and object-oriented analysis and design. These are very important activities, with whole books devoted to each topic. Therefore, in the resource list in Appendix A, you will find our favorite books on these topics.

We have used one example, an order-processing system for a mail order company, throughout the book. This allows us to maintain consistency and build up a reasonably complex example. Parts of the solution are given in the various chapters to illustrate the concepts.

This book is presented as a sequence of steps, though life is never that simple. Each part will contribute to the rest until the system is complete. So if a section says to create an architecture, do what you can at that time, using what you currently know. You will add to it and refine it based on knowledge gained while working through the process.

You don't have to read the whole book before starting with use cases. Chapters 1 through 5 give the basics of working with use cases. We recommend that everyone reads those chapters. Chapter 6 covers architecture and mapping use cases into the architecture. Chapter 7 covers documenting use cases. Chapter 8 covers project planning with use cases, and Chapter 9 covers reviewing the use case documents. Chapter 10 goes into moving from use cases to OOAD.

Ultimately, use cases are about documenting your system. Plan on doing a lot of writing. Appendix A provides a list of books we reference throughout the text, as well as other books we have found useful when developing projects. Appendix B shows the document templates used. These provide an example and a starting point for your own project. Modify them as needed to work with your project.

△ ▽ △ ▽ △

In October of 1995, Rational Software Corporation merged with Objective Systems. Among other things, this merger brought with it Ivar Jacobson and his use cases. In February 1996, I wrote and delivered the first use case course for Rational, which combined use cases with the object-oriented methodologies of Grady Booch and Jim Rumbaugh. Since that time, I have taught and run workshops on use cases with many of Rational's customers, as well as customers of my consulting company, Wyyzzk Training and Consulting. As I have taught them, so they have taught me. This book came out of what I've learned through the workshops.

Acknowledgments

Thanks to:

My parents, Phil and Joan Schneider. Their love and faith give me the confidence to reach for the stars and the persistence to succeed.

My professors at Southern Illinois University, Edwardsville, in particular Dr. Nadine Verderber, Dr. Greg Stephen, and Dr. Eric Sturley. The education I received has proved to be a firm foundation on which I could build knowledge and skills.

Dr. Ivar Jacobson for the original work on use cases. I've built on the foundations he defined. Thanks also for his comments on the book in its early stages. His comments got me past a stuck point at a critical time.

My colleagues at Rational Software Corporation for their encouragement and support, particularly the men and women in the North American Field Organization, the International Field Organization, and Technical Support. Each one is an outstanding engineer, always willing to share with the rest what he or she has learned. This free exchange of ideas has been invaluable for maturing the processes we all teach—use cases, OOAD, and OOPM. In particular I want to thank my former team, Deborah Bell, Sue Mickel, and Jean-Pierre Schoch, for their support and encouragement.

Neal Reizer, Bill Fairfield, and Garth Andrews for their support and encouragement and my customers and students, who taught me much while I was mentoring them.

Karin Palmkvist who helped us tremendously by doing a final review of the manuscript.

Bob and Norma Hughes for mowing our lawn when we got too busy with the book to do it. And we didn't even ask!

Special thanks to Dr. James Rumbaugh. He has helped me through the publishing process, giving advice and encouragement along the way. His intercession led to Addison-Wesley reviewing and publishing this book.

Many thanks to our distinguished reviewers. They worked as hard as we did to make this book happen.

- Kurt Bittner—Rational Software Corporation
- Rosemary Brinko—American Management Systems
- Susan Burk—American Management Systems
- Lois Delcambre—Professor, Computer Science and Engineering Department, Oregon Graduate Institute
- Benjamin Godfrey
- Kelli A. Houston—Rational Software Corporation
- John Sunda Hsia
- Dean Larsen
- Jas S. Madhur—Rational Software Corporation
- Phil Price—Qualcomm
- Arthur J. Riel
- Somboon Supakkul

Speaking of hard workers, we were most fortunate to be working with J. Carter Shanklin, Angela Buenning, Rachel Beavers, and Krysia Bebick at Addison Wesley Longman. Our most heartfelt thanks for all your support and encouragement. You guys did all the tough work to make this book a reality. Special thanks to Marilyn Rash, and her team of editing and typesetting experts, who made sure this book got through production.

Last, but not least, thank you to Jason Winters for his love, support, and encouragement. He is the storyteller who brought the book to life. His unique insights brought clarity to a sometimes difficult subject.

Geri Schneider Winters
Santa Clara, California

Chapter 1

Getting Started

Use cases are used to describe the outwardly visible requirements of a system. They are used in the requirements analysis phase of a project and contribute to test plans and user guides. They are used to create and validate a proposed design and to ensure it meets all requirements. Use cases also are used when creating a project schedule, helping to plan what goes into each release.

This book will give practical guidelines for applying use cases to a project. We will cover a project from its initial inception ("Hey! How about. . . .") to just before we actually start to build it. We also will look at applying use cases in testing the system code and creating user manuals.

In this book we'll look at use cases from many viewpoints, showing how they contribute to the architecture, scheduling, requirements, testing, and documentation of a project. We'll look at the system from the user's point of view, discuss issues such as boundaries, interfaces, and scoping, and look at how to break a really large system into manageable chunks. We also will look at who would be interested in the documentation you'll be writing and what to look for in a review. We need to consider things such as how to build flexibility into a system, making a build-versus-buy decision, and how to turn the documents into an object-oriented design.

This book does not contain in-depth details about software architecture, project planning, testing, process, or methodology. Instead, you will find a listing of books we like on these topics in Resources (see Appendix A). There are a number of good books on these topics; the resource list gives you just a starting point.

AN ITERATIVE SOFTWARE PROCESS

Use cases can be used in many processes. Our favorite is a process that is iterative and risk driven. It works well with use cases and object-oriented methodologies. It helps identify and address risks early in the process, leading to more robust and better quality systems. We will give a very brief description of the process here, showing where use cases fit into the process. Subsequent chapters will go into more detail on how use cases are used at each phase.

This iterative, risk-driven process is divided into four primary phases: inception, elaboration, construction, and transition.

During the inception phase you will determine the scope of the project and create a business case for it. At the end of the inception phase you should be able to answer the question, Does it make good business sense for us to continue with this project?

During the elaboration phase you will do requirements analysis and risk analysis, develop a baseline architecture, and create a plan for the construction phase.

During the construction phase you will progress through a series of iterations. Each iteration will include analysis, design, implementation, and testing.

During the transition phase you will complete the things that make what you developed into a product. This can include beta testing, performance tuning, and creating additional documentation such as training, user guides, and sales kits. You will create a plan for rolling out the product to the user community, whether internal or external.

So where do use cases fit into all this? In the inception phase, high-level use cases are developed to help scope out the project. What should be included in this project, and what belongs to another project? What can we realistically accomplish given our schedule and budget?

In the elaboration phase, you will develop more detailed use cases. These will contribute to the risk analysis and the baseline architecture. The use cases will be used to create the plan for the construction phase.

In the construction phase, use cases will be used as a starting point for design and for developing test plans. More detailed use cases may be developed as part of the analysis of each iteration. Use cases provide some of the requirements that have to be satisfied for each iteration.

In the transition phase, use cases can be used to develop user guides and training.

AN EXAMPLE PROJECT

Throughout this book we will use an example project. We will work through all the techniques using the same example. The notation we will use is the Unified Modeling Language, which is outlined in Appendix C.

The example we will be following is for an order-processing system for a mail order company. So let's start at the very beginning, when four friends gathered around a table after dinner and someone got an idea.

"This is crazy!" Dennis exclaimed, sitting down next to Tara, almost spilling his coffee.

"What is?" Lisa asked, sitting down with Gus and her own cup of mocha.

"The fact that I can't find a single supplier that will give me reasonable service and parts without all the headaches! I've got one supplier who has great service and I like dealing with him. But he takes three weeks to get me even the simplest order! And the other one, oh, they're something else. Sure, I can get orders within three days, but half the time the orders are wrong, and when I call them back about it, they make it sound like it's my fault! It's almost as if they are TRYING to make me go elsewhere."

"Yes, I know what you mean," Lisa said. "I've had my own problems with mail order companies. You'd think they would pay more attention to their customers!"

"I really think I could do a better job myself. I sure know a lot about what not to do."

This had been a common complaint from Dennis in the last several months, and by now the group was well acquainted with it. Tara suddenly smiled and piped up with "Why don't you start one?" "Start one what?" Dennis muttered into in his coffee.

"Start a mail order company! What would you do to fix the problems you've seen?"

"Well, it seems like automating the order processing would help a lot. It would also let me run the company myself for a while. But I don't know anything about software."

At this point, Gus joined the conversation. "You need to plan it out. I learned a method in my OO class we could use. And we could help! By putting us and all of our experiences together, we could figure out how to use our different skills in the right places and work out the sections we don't know!"

"OO? What's that? You know I'm not a programmer. I don't know anything about programming languages."

"No, OO isn't about a programming language. It's a way of thinking about a problem, a way of modeling and breaking it down into identifiable objects so you can work with them. It really doesn't matter what the problem is, whether it's a programming problem or a problem like starting a new business. It's just an approach on how you look at it."

"Hmmm. . . ." mused Dennis, liking the idea the more he thought about it. "And you would all be willing to help?"

"Sure!"

"Why not?"

"Sounds like fun!"

"Well. . . Okay! So, Gus, where do we start with this all-dancing-all-singing magical OO process?"

Before getting into writing use cases, you have to gather some information that will provide a starting point. This is part of the inception phase of the Rational Unified Process. The information we collect includes a project description, market factors that affect our project, risk factors for our project, and assumptions we are making. The rest of this chapter will touch on all those sources of information.

THE PROJECT DESCRIPTION

So you have an idea for a project. The next step is to write out a description of what you plan to do. It sounds simple, and it can be. But the larger the group you have writing this description, the longer it will take and the more complex it will be. It is best to have just a couple of people write out a brief, but complete, description of the project.

The project description should range in size from one short paragraph for a small project, up to no more than a couple of pages for a really large project. This is not a description of the requirements, but a description of the project in general.

The biggest mistake made at this point is not writing the description. Usually this is because everybody thinks they know what the project is about, so why write it down. We have spent several days in meetings while the project team argued about what a one-paragraph description should say. Until you write it out, you can't be sure everyone agrees on the same project description.

"So let's get started. We need to write out a description of order processing in normal everyday language. This will become the problem statement, a way to start getting the requirements for the project."

"Why do we need to write it out? We're all familiar with ordering products from mail order companies. This seems too formal for such a simple problem."

"Well, we should write it all down to make sure everyone has the same idea. Even if you were working alone, it's still a good idea to write it down so you don't leave out something important. Besides, it'll give us someplace to start, and we can add to it as we go along. Here, I'll start."

Problem Description

We are developing order-processing software for a mail order company called National Widgets, which is a reseller of products purchased from various suppliers.

Twice a year the company publishes a catalog of products, which is mailed to customers and other interested people.

"You think twice a year is good? What if our products change faster than that?"

"Remember, this is just to start us off. We will add to it and change it as we get farther along and understand more about what's going on. Let's keep going."

More Requirements

Customers purchase products by submitting a list of products with payment to National Widgets. National Widgets fills the order and ships the products to the customer's address.

The order-processing software will track the order from the time it is received until the product is shipped.

National Widgets will provide quick service. They should be able to ship a customer's order by the fastest, most efficient means possible.

"Great! That looks like us! Now, what else should we do?"

What have our friends done right? They kept the description brief, talking about what they want to accomplish, not how to do it. They wrote down the elements important to them: It's a catalog company, a reseller, not a manufacturer; it provides quick service; and the software is used throughout the process to track orders. These are the key characteristics of their project. They didn't worry about making their description perfect. If something were important that they NOT do, they would have written that down as well. They got a basic description that they agree on but that may need to be modified later. However, the key characteristics should not change.

STARTING RISK ANALYSIS

Now that you have a description, the next step is to write down other things you know about your project. You are looking for marketing factors that will influence your project, good or bad, and things that are required that may not have appeared in the description. We will use these with the problem statement to create use cases, other requirements, and risk factors. Here are some things to consider:

- Who or what the competition is
- What technologies you are depending on, such as:
  - Web
  - Object databases
  - Power PC chip

- Market trends that influence your project
- Number of expected users
- Future trends you are depending on, such as:
  - More home offices
  - More small companies

- Number of transactions per time frame
- Expected duration of some functionality
- Legacy systems you have to interface with, such as:
  - Software
  - Business processes
  - Data stores, databases

For our mail order company we can create a list of market factors based on personal experience.

Mail Order Market Factors

In most households, all adults work at least part time. They have less time available for shopping, so they usually are willing to pay for conveniences such as having purchases delivered.

Web shopping and home shopping networks are popular and are competitors in this market.

Other mail order companies provide 24-hour order takers, delivery times ranging from overnight to two weeks, gift wrap, and volume discounts.

Be creative as you make this list. Brainstorm a lot. Put down just about anything you can think of. Put down the wildly unlikely as well as things that will probably happen. The idea at this stage is to look at the project from many viewpoints. This will help solidify your ideas. Look at some books on marketing trends for ideas. What are competing companies doing right or doing wrong?

You also need to consider risk factors in your project. You need to include things that can go wrong. Writing down only the things that you'd *like* to happen is a sure recipe for disaster. Far better to think of how it can go wrong so you can plan on it, than to wander along and get surprised.

You also need to include things like being wildly successful. Sometimes you'll find things actually can go wrong if you are too successful. For example, what would happen to National Widgets if, in the first month, they get 4,000 calls? We now have to handle multiple order takers and large amounts of data. Presuming the company can handle this surge, can the software handle it? The company could lose business if the software is not up to the demands placed on it, possibly getting a bad reputation because of it. Our friends will write this down as one of their risks.

Here are some things to consider as possible risk factors (see also Exhibit 1-1):

- Lack of user acceptance
- Dependence on a technology that changes
- Not fast enough to market
- Too many users
- Team not experienced enough
- Too short a schedule
- Too-fast company growth
- Too fast to market
- Supplier can't or won't deliver product we depend on

Our risk factors for the order-processing project take into consideration the inexperience of the team, system failure, and the needs of the market.

National Widgets Risk Factors

- Some of the people designing the software are inexperienced.
- How can we prevent lost orders on system failure?
- The system has to be easy for nontechnical people to use.
- Can we be successful if we don't support a Web interface?
- What if the system is immediately flooded with orders?
- How do we handle many simultaneous users in different parts of the company?
- How do we handle the database crashing?

Take this list of risks and the list of project factors, eliminate extremes such as a comet crashing into your company and putting you out of business or the sun failing to rise, and prioritize the rest. This prioritized list you've created is your first risk analysis. All the things you've listed here put you at risk for not completing your project. The more serious items are listed first, with less severe risks at the bottom of the list. The high risk factors must be addressed if you expect your project to succeed.

Remember that this is just a starting point and that you'll be adding to it as you continue!

As part of your risk list, put together and maintain a list of assumptions. These are decisions you make with little or no hard data. You may need to pick one way of doing something based on gut feel or experience. Record that decision and why you made it. This list should be reviewed regularly. Some things will remain as assumptions. For others, you will be able to get hard data on which to base your decisions. Remove things that are no longer assumptions and add the new assumptions you've made.

Let's go back and see how the group members are doing with their lists.

"Okay, it's been a busy evening. Let's see what we've gotten out of it." Gus handed around the lists shown in Exhibit 1.1.

Exhibit 1-1   Order-Processing Problem Statement

Problem Description

- We are developing order-processing software for a mail order company called National Widgets, which is a reseller of products purchased from various suppliers.
- Twice a year the company publishes a catalog of products, which is mailed to customers and other interested people.
- Customers purchase products by submitting a list of products with payment to National Widgets. National Widgets fills the order and ships the products to the customer's address.
- The order-processing software will track the order from the time it is received until the product is shipped.
- National Widgets will provide quick service. They should be able to ship a customer's order by the fastest, most efficient means possible.
- Customers may return items for restocking but will sometimes pay a fee.

Assumptions

- An electronic interface, such as the Web, would be good for some customers.
- We expect to use multiple shipping companies and insured methods.

Risk Factors

- Some of the people designing the software are inexperienced.
- How can we prevent lost orders on system failure?
- The system has to be easy for nontechnical people to use.
- Can we be successful if we don't support a Web interface?
- What if the system is immediately flooded with orders?
- How do we handle many simultaneous users in different parts of the company?
- How do we handle the database crashing?

Exhibit 1-1 Order-Processing Problem Statement (*Continued*)

Market Factors

- In most households, all adults work at least part time. They have less time available for shopping, so are usually willing to pay for conveniences such as having purchases delivered.
- Web shopping and home shopping networks are popular and are competitors in this market.
- Other mail order companies provide 24-hour order takers, delivery times ranging from overnight to two weeks, gift wrap, and volume discounts.

"Wow," was Dennis' comment. "We sure can fail in a lot of ways. But how has this helped us define the software? So far, all it's done is make me worry that we forgot something."

"Don't worry, Dennis. We're just getting started. We want to find things that could make us fail now so we can fix the problems rather than getting surprised by them later."

CHAPTER REVIEW

Table 1-1 shows deliverables you should have complete at this point. Your risk analysis should include known risks, other known market factors, and assumptions you have made about the project.

These are just preliminary versions, showing what you know right now. You will modify these things as you learn more about your project. The next chapter covers using use cases to find the boundaries of the system and the scope of the project.

Table 1-1 Inception Phase Deliverables

Complete	Deliverables
✔	Project description
✔	Risk analysis
	Use case diagram
	Description of actors and use cases
	Project proposal

Chapter 2

Identifying System Boundaries

By now you have a high-level overview of the project and an idea of the risks you are facing. Let's define a couple of terms we have been using before going on. The system is whatever you are planning to create. It could be software, hardware, or processes. The project encompasses all the things you do to build a system. So it will include things such as planning, scheduling, and documentation.

The next step in our process is to clearly identify the boundaries of the system. This means finding out what things are inside your system (you have to worry about creating them) and what are outside your system (you don't have to create them but you have to worry about interfacing with them). We also will be concerned with scoping the project. This involves defining what parts of the system you will create within a certain time period, on a certain budget.

Some system boundaries are very easy to define, such as a person interacting with a program. Most likely you won't have to worry about creating the person. The program, however, is clearly within your project. Others have fuzzier borders.

System Boundary Example

What is the boundary of this system?

National Widgets will need to ship orders to customers. Shipping needs to include packaging and labeling orders, weighing them, and determining postage based on shipping method, speed of delivery, insurance, weight, destination, and so on.

Should our system include the printing of mailing labels and calculating postage?

You will find the boundaries of your system by identifying the actors and the use cases.

IDENTIFYING ACTORS

We'll start off by identifying the actors in our system. Actors are anything that interfaces with your system. Some examples are people, other software, hardware devices, data stores, or networks. Each actor defines a particular role. Each entity outside your system may be represented by one or more actors. So one physical person may be represented by several actors because that person takes on different roles with regard to the system. Or several physical people might be represented by one actor because they all take on the same role with regard to the system.

For example, a person, Mary Smith, is a customer of National Widgets. But she also is an employee of National Widgets. The person Mary Smith is represented by two actors, Customer and Employee, because they represent two different roles with regard to the company. John Forsythe also is a customer of National Widgets. He and Mary Smith are represented by the same actor, Customer, because they take on the same role with regard to the company.

Actors always are external to your system. They are never a part of your system. To help find actors in your system, you can ask yourself:

- Who uses the system?
- Who installs the system?
- Who starts up the system?
- Who maintains the system?
- Who shuts down the system?
- What other systems use this system?
- Who gets information from this system?
- Who provides information to the system?
- Does anything happen automatically at a preset time?

Gus and his friends have had some time to get the general feel of what they wanted the software to do. Now it's time to put some of those ideas to use.

"Well," Gus said, "Here we are again. That was a great dinner, Tara! Thanks!"

"You're welcome, Gus. I guess Dennis didn't notice. . . he's got that faraway look in his eyes. Hello? Dennis? Hey!"

"Huh? Oh! Sorry, gang. I was just thinking about what we ended up doing last week. I still don't see how it's helped us so far, other than giving a very basic description of what we are doing. Don't we need a lot more details? I just don't get it."

"Well," Gus said, "You're right. We're ready for the next step in the process—figuring out who we interact with."

"Don't we interact with customers?" Lisa asked, as she sat down with her coffee.

"Yes, we do! And that's why we call the customer an actor. In fact, the customer will be the first actor that we write down. Who else? Tara?"

"Well, since we have to get orders from us to our customers, we'll need to interact with someone like Dolphin Mail or USPS."

"Good!" Gus exclaimed. "Now let's put that down on paper.

Dennis, glancing at the drawing [Exhibit 2-1], said, "Hey! That guy even looks like one of our customers!"

"Yes, that helps us keep in mind who's doing what. The stick men are our actors. What's wrong, Lisa?"

"Why is there only one shipping company? Won't we work with a lot of companies?"

"That's right. But fortunately, we don't show each person or each shipping company as a separate actor. For example, we might use Federal Express, DHL, or Dolphin Mail for deliveries. Because they all interface with us the same way, we can show them as one actor."

"There he goes, talking 'interfaces' again. . . ," Lisa muttered.

"Well, it's true, they ARE using the same interface. For example, what if we had to have a different type of order form for each customer? Wouldn't *that* be a headache!"

"It sure would! Okay, you've convinced me."

"Are we really interfacing with the shipping companies? That would be only if they used our order-processing system directly, right?"

"Say, that's right. Wouldn't it really be a shipping clerk at National Widgets using the software?"

"And our customer should be a customer service rep."

"What about the Web? Don't we want to interact with customers directly?"

Gus stepped in. "Let's go ahead and put them all down [see Exhibit 2-2]. We can change this later if we decide to do or not do some of those things."

Exhibit 2-1 Sample Actors

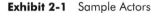

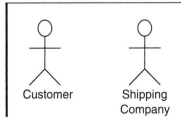

Customer   Shipping
Company

Exhibit 2-2 More Order-Processing Actors

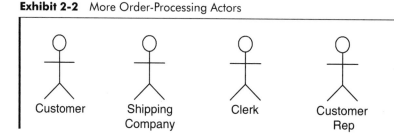

IDENTIFYING USE CASES
===================

The next step is to go through all of the actors and identify use cases for each one. Use cases describe the things actors want the system to do, such as querying the status of an existing order. In the UML, a use case is always started by an actor. We have found it useful on occasion to initiate use cases from inside the system, but this is rare.

Ask yourself:

- What functions will the actor want from the system?
- Does the system store information? What actors will create, read, update, or delete that information?
- Does the system need to notify an actor about changes in its internal state?
- Are there any external events the system must know about? What actor informs the system about those events?

Other kinds of use cases to consider are start up, shut down, diagnostics, installation, training, and changing a business process. A common one that many people forget is maintenance. How are you going to repair the system? Will you have to shut it down or can you do your maintenance on it while still using the system? When considering these and other questions, determine whether these functions are handled by your system. All of the use cases together will describe the complete functionality of the system from the user's point of view.

"OK," Gus said. "Any more ideas for actors? No? Well, that's okay. We have enough information to get started with the next step, which is identifying use cases. We can add more actors later as we find them."

"So," Dennis asked, "what is a use case?"

"It's a way actors use our company," Gus replied. "So what do our customers want from us?"

"Hmm . . ." Tara mused, "Well, I would assume they want to place an order. If they don't, we won't be in business long enough to worry about anything else!"

"Great. What else do our customers want?"

"They check the status of their order."

"They have to get our catalog to know what to order!"

"They cancel an order."

"Pessimist."

"They return stuff they have purchased."

"Hey, what happens after they order? Don't they have to receive the order?"

"Whoa! Slow down! I can't write that fast!" Gus quickly jotted down notes, and soon was ready to go on. "Who asked about what happens after they order? Lisa? Okay, what does happen after they order?"

"Well, I would imagine we'd ship the order to them. Hey! Does that mean that we need to notify the shipping company when an order is ready for delivery?"

"Very good!" Gus said, "That's exactly what it means. So now we have to add that use case for the shipping company actor. Let's add the use cases to our diagram [see Exhibit 2-3]. We can use a single actor to show the starting point of many operations, such as checking the status of an order or canceling it. The use cases are represented by ovals on the diagram. The boundary of the system is represented by a rectangle surrounding the use cases. Actors are outside the rectangle because they are outside the system. Solid lines connect actors to their use cases."

"Hey!" Tara pointed at the page. "Do we really want the supplier interfacing directly with our software?"

"Maybe we can get the software to automatically place an order with a supplier when our stock is low."

"Shouldn't the inventory system do that?"

"Are we writing that too?"

"No way. It's enough to just process orders. We can buy an inventory system to use."

"Isn't that an actor then?"

"You're right. How about accounting systems?"

"Sure. Buy that too."

"I have a question for you, Gus," Lisa said. "How do you know where to draw the circles versus the actor? Why don't we have an actor in place of the Deliver Product use case? Doesn't the Place Order use case interact with it? Wouldn't that make Deliver Product an actor?"

"Not exactly. You see, one of the basic rules for something to be declared an actor is that we don't have control over it. If we don't have control over something, then it's an outside influence, as in outside our process, and that means it's an actor. If we have full control of it, like we do between the Place Order module and the Deliver Product module, then it's internal to our system. We don't need to define the interface between Place Order and Deliver Product yet because nobody on the outside can see it. Only the interface between Deliver Product and a Shipping Company is visible."

"Got it! Let's keep going, because I've got some more use cases for you."

Exhibit 2-3 Order-Processing Use Cases

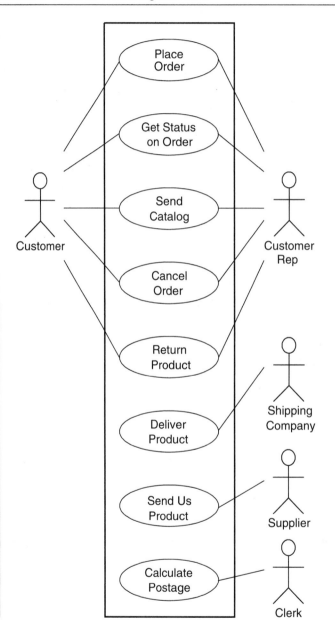

DESCRIBING ACTORS AND USE CASES

Each actor needs a descriptive name and a brief description that is one or two sentences long. This will define the actor's role with regard to the system.

Order-Processing Actor Descriptions

Customer – a person who orders products from National Widgets

Customer rep – an employee of National Widgets who processes customer requests

Shipping company – USPS, UPS, DHL, FedEx, DM, and so on

Clerk – an employee of National Widgets who packages, labels, and ships orders

Inventory system – software that tracks the company inventory

Accounting system – software that keeps the company books

Each use case will need a descriptive name. You may also want to include a one- or two-sentence description, if the name doesn't tell enough about the functionality of the use case.

Order-Processing Use Cases

From a customer – place order, send catalog, get status on order, return product, cancel order, register complaint

From a customer rep – place order, send catalog, get status on order, return product, cancel order, register complaint

To shipping companies – packages ready for delivery

From clerk – print mailing label, calculate postage

To inventory system – give product information, update product quantities

From inventory system – back-ordered items received

To accounting system – charge account, credit account

In the process of identifying and defining actors and use cases, you are determining your system boundaries—what is inside the system (use cases) and what is outside (actors). Record this information in a use case diagram. Remember, this is only the first cut! Throughout this process, we will be constantly adding to and refining this diagram.

Review your system description, market factors, risk factors, assumptions, and any other requirements you are aware of. Are all the users of the system represented as actors? Are all the system functions represented as use cases?

What Gus and his friends have come up with for a use case diagram at this point is represented in Exhibit 2-4, parts *a* and *b*.

As can be seen, they have come up with things that are done by actors representing the customer, customer rep, shipping company, clerk, inventory system, and accounting system.

What if the use case diagram is too big and messy? As we did in Exhibit 2-4, you could create several use case diagrams. Each diagram might represent a major area of functionality in your system. Or you could have one per actor or one per use case. At various points in the project, you need to compare these diagrams to remove redundancies and keep them consistent. Automated Computer-Aided Software Engineering (CASE) tools can help with this process.

HANDLING TIME

In some systems, there are activities that take place at certain times. For example, we might run payroll every Friday, or print a system report every day at midnight. There are essentially two ways to handle time in use cases.

One method of handling time in your use cases is to treat it as an actor. Then, the time actor can initiate the use case to run the payroll, or print the system report.

The second method of handling time is to treat time as part of the system. In this method, a use case starts itself at some time. The actor that interacts with the use case is one that will receive the output of the use case. You might define a paymaster actor to receive the output of the run payroll use case. Possibly a printer actor receives the output of the print system report use case.

POTENTIAL BOUNDARY PROBLEMS

What if some of your requirements should be handled by one of the actors? In this case, you need to determine if that actor is really a part of your system. If the actor is not part of the system, then the requirements cannot be a part of the system. In this case, the requirements must be communicated to the actor or whoever is designing the system represented by that actor. Otherwise, the requirements need to be redefined so it is clear they are a part of the system.

If you decide the actor should be part of your system, look at the description. Perhaps the actor or its role needs to be redefined to make the system boundary clearer. If the actor becomes a part of your system, what about use cases that were associated with that actor? Who or what interacts with those use cases now? Maybe the use cases need to be redefined.

Exhibit 2-4a Order-Processing Use Cases

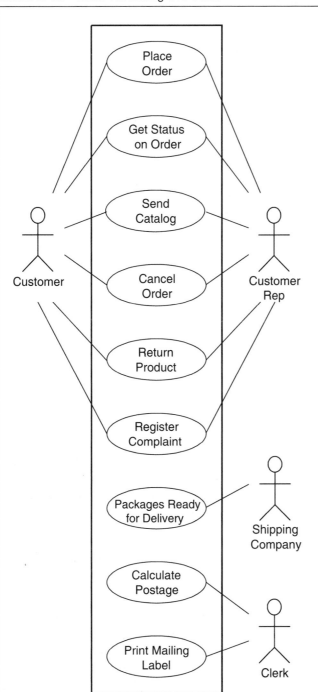

Exhibit 2-4b Order-Processing Use Cases

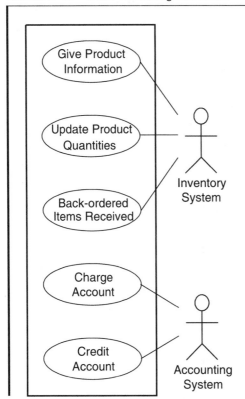

Who Handles This Requirement?

National Widgets decides they need to provide insurance on the packages they ship. Who will provide this insurance? Will National Widgets provide the insurance, or will the shipping companies provide the insurance? Will the insurance be tracked in the order-processing system or calculated by the system? How does the system decide which kind of insurance to use, or should it?

What if you find new requirements as you go through the process of identifying actors and use cases? Ask yourself if the requirements are inside or outside your system. Some of the questions to ask yourself when you find new requirements are:

- Are these requirements necessary for this system?
- Are these requirements something this system would logically do?
- How do the new requirements affect our current risk analysis?
- Can these requirements be handled by one of the current actors to our system? In other words, is someone else responsible for them?

- Are these requirements something our customers would expect our system to do?
- Would these requirements differentiate our product in the marketplace?

Defining a clear boundary for your system may be very difficult. That would indicate your system is not well defined. If you expect to deliver a system on time and on budget, you must have a good project description with well-defined system boundaries. It is worth spending the time doing this work up front. Otherwise, you will struggle with it throughout the lifetime of the project.

SCOPING THE PROJECT

Having determined the boundaries of your system, you need to decide on a scope for your project. A project has a particular begin and end date, and some amount of money that can be spent to accomplish the goals of the project. Do you intend to build the whole system in the current project? If not, you need to clearly define the pieces of the system that will be included and those that will not. Use some method of prioritizing the requirements so you can verify that everything that must be included in the system is there, and you can ensure that things that are not necessary are not worked on.

Some of the requirements you have identified will be obviously necessary—the basic processes of the system. These should be marked some way, such as Required, or Must Have. Other requirements are important, but not vital. These could be marked as Important, or Should Have. Others would be nice to have and could be marked as Nice, or Could Have. The rest are pie in the sky, something we are dreaming of but probably won't get to this time around. They could be marked as Future, or Would Like To Have.

When prioritizing requirements, you also have to consider the risks and market factors you have identified. So Must Haves are not just based on technical necessity, but might also address risks in the marketplace. For National Widgets, this might mean that a Web interface is a Must Have for the order-processing system because every other mail order company offers it. This feature is required just to stay level with the competition.

Choose some way of prioritizing your requirements and use it consistently. Consider a requirements management tool to store this information for later retrieval and report generation.

When scoping your project, you need to estimate what could realistically be accomplished in the time frame allowed, with the budget and resources allowed. All Must Have requirements will have to be included, and most Should Haves. What else can you afford to include?

As you work through the process of defining the boundaries of the system and later as you detail use cases, you may find more requirements for your system. In going through the process you have determined that these requirements are within the boundary of your system. But are they within the scope of your project? Ask yourself these questions:

- Can we afford to add these new requirements on our schedule and budget?
- Should we add a later, second version of the system and address these new requirements then?
- If we have to add them now, can we move other requirements to the later version?

Is This Requirement in Scope?

National Widgets has looked at the market and noticed that Web commerce is really popular. Should they have Web pages, an on-line catalog, and electronic ordering in the first release of the order-processing software? How important is this requirement?

Things that are nice to have but are not required should be considered for a later phase of this system or for a later project. Remember that the hardest part of a project is to get to release 1.0. Going from 1.0 to 1.1 is a lot easier.

CHAPTER REVIEW

At this point you should have a clearly defined boundary for your system as well as a clearly defined scope for your project. Some things to ask yourself are:

- Are the system requirements all represented by use cases? If not, verify that these requirements are internal to your system and can't be seen by the actors. These kinds of requirements don't appear on a use case diagram.
- Do all the actors and use cases have descriptive names? Do those that need further explanation have short descriptions?
- Are the system boundaries and the project scope clearly defined? If not, this becomes a major risk to your project. Clear this up as soon as possible. If questions cannot be answered, make a decision and record it in your list of assumptions.
- Are all areas of uncertainty recorded in the list of assumptions?

Table 2-1 Inception Phase Deliverables

Complete	Deliverables
✔	Project description
✔	Risk analysis
✔	Use case diagram
✔	Description of actors and use cases
✔	Project proposal

Go back and update the project description, risks, assumptions, and so on, as needed to reflect things you have learned while defining the system boundaries.

Table 2-1 shows the deliverables you should have complete. This completes the information gathering for the inception phase. Other activities of this phase, such as writing a proposal and creating a business justification for the project, are beyond the scope of this book.

Our friends who are starting the mail order company have decided the project is feasible and will go ahead with it. We hope the same is true for your project. We will continue in the next chapter with writing detailed use case descriptions.

Chapter 3

Primary Scenarios

We have completed the inception phase of our project by deciding that we are going to do this project. It looks feasible to management and marketing. Now we need to spend more time adding details to the technical parts of the documentation.

During the elaboration phase you will spend time adding details to the requirements of the project. You want to finish this phase of the project having confidence that technically it can be completed within a certain time frame and budget. The documents you will be creating include detailed use cases and a project plan. You might also create one or more prototypes to test some particular piece of the system.

THE COMPLETE USE CASE

Each use case must include details about what has to be done to accomplish the functionality of the use case. We need to consider the basic functionality, any alternatives, error conditions, anything that must be true before starting the use case, and anything that must be true on exiting the use case. The use case may include conditionals, branching, and loops. The Rational Unified Process gives a basic format for a use case, including precondition, flow of events (basic and alternatives), and postcondition. Let's look at an example of a possible use case for an order-processing system.

Place Order

Precondition: A valid user has logged into the system.

Flow of Events:

Basic Path

1. The use case starts when the customer selects Place Order.
2. The customer enters his or her name and address.
3. If the customer enters only the zip code, the system will supply the city and state.
4. The customer will enter product codes for the desired products.
5. The system will supply a product description and price for each item.
6. The system will keep a running total of items ordered as they are entered.
7. The customer will enter credit card payment information.
8. The customer will select Submit.
9. The system will verify the information, save the order as pending, and forward payment information to the accounting system.
10. When payment is confirmed, the order is marked Confirmed, an order ID is returned to the customer, and the use case ends.

Alternative Paths

In step 9, if any information is incorrect, the system will prompt the customer to correct the information.

Postcondition: The order has been saved in the system and marked confirmed.

The format of this use case works very well for relatively simple use cases. Everything you need to know about the use case is in one place. We can continue refining this, adding branching or alternative flows to show error handling or other alternatives. Let's look at the parts that make up a use case in a little more detail.

Pre- and Postconditions

Pre- and postconditions indicate what comes before and after the use case. They tell what state the system must be in at the start of the use case (precondition), or what state the system must be in at the end of the use case (postcondition). The postcondition must be true no matter which branch or alternative is followed for the use case.

For an example, we will presume that our order-processing system automatically sends sales tax to the government once every quarter for products sold that quarter. We are simplifying the example by ignoring the fact that sales tax probably will have to be sent to more than one state or locality. We simply want to send in a sales tax payment if it is the end of the quarter. We have to be positive the taxes were credited because the government imposes severe penalties on companies that do not pay their sales tax on time (see Exhibit 3-1).

Exhibit 3-1   Pre- and Postcondition Example

Deposit Sales Tax Use Case

Precondition: It is the end of one of National Widgets business quarters

Flow of Events:

1. The system determines the amount of sales tax collected for the quarter.
2. The system sends an electronic payment of sales tax to the government.

Postcondition: The government has deposited our taxes and updated our records.

Note that the postcondition must be true, no matter what. If our electronic payment does not go through for some reason, National Widgets is still responsible for paying the sales tax on time. No matter what errors happen, the postcondition still must be true.

Flow of Events

The *flow of events* is a series of declarative statements listing the steps of a use case. Alternatives can be shown using branching or by listing them under the Alternative Paths. Typically, we use an if statement to indicate alternatives. We have already seen examples of this, such as in Find Order (Exhibit 3-2).

In the Place Order use case, we showed an alternative in the Alternative Paths section of the use case rather than writing it with an if statement. We also show an if statement in step 3.

Use repetition when you need to repeat a step or a set of steps multiple times. Indicate clearly where the repetition starts and ends. Also indicate

Exhibit 3-2   Branching Example

Find Order Use Case

Flow of Events:
1. The user may enter an order ID, customer ID, or customer name.
2. The user will press Find.
3. **If the user entered an order ID**
    a) the system will display that order.
4. **If the user entered a cutomer name or customer ID**
    a) the system will return a list of all orders for that customer.
    b) The user will select one order from the list.
    c) The system will display that order.

Exhibit 3-3 Repetition Example with for

Place Order Use Case

Flow of Events:

1. The use case starts when the customer selects Place Order.

2. The customer enters his or her name and address.

3. The customer will enter product codes for products to be ordered.

4. **For each product code entered**

   a) **the system will supply a product description and price.**

   b) **the system will add the price of the item to the total.**

end

5. The customer will enter credit card payment information.

6. The customer will select Submit.

7. The system will verify the information, save the order as pending, and forward payment information to the accounting system.

8. When payment is confirmed, the order is marked confirmed, an order ID is returned to the customer, and the use case ends.

---

clearly how you will end the repetition. The repetition may end because you have gotten to the end of a set of things, or there may be some condition that causes the repetition to stop. Typically we use a for or while to indicate repetition.

We really should indicate repetition in our Place Order use case because the user can enter more than one product on a single order. It's implied in the current text, but it is better to make the repetition explicit (see Exhibit 3-3).

Exhibit 3-4 is the same example using while instead of for. They do the same job and look almost identical in text. Use whichever is easier for you and your team to read and understand.

Alternative Paths

An alternative path gives the alternatives to the basic path. It can be used in place of branching when the alternative is somewhat complex. The alternative path is particularly good for showing things that can happen at any time—something that interrupts the normal flow of events. This could be used to indicate the situation where a user decides to cancel placing an order partway through the use case. Another example (see Exhibit 3-5) is when a user requests context-specific help during some activity. For example, during the

Exhibit 3-4 Repetition Example with `while`

Place Order Use Case

Flow of Events:

1. The use case starts when the customer selects Place Order.

2. The customer enters his or her name and address.

3. If the customer enters only the zip code, the system will suply the city and state.

4. **While the customer enters product codes**

    a) **the system will supply a product description and price.**

    b) **the system will add the price of the item to the total.**

end

5. The customer will enter credit card payment information.

6. The customer will select Submit.

7. The system will verify the information, save the order as pending, and forward payment information to the accounting system.

8. When payment is confirmed, the order is marked confirmed, an order ID is returned to the customer, and the use case ends.

Exhibit 3-5 Alternative Flow of Events Example

Place Order Use Case

Flow of Events:

Basic Path

1. The use case starts when the customer selects Place Order.

2. The customer enters his or her name and address.

3. While the customer enters product codes

    a) the system will supply a product description and price.

    b) the system will add the price of the item to the total.

end

4. The customer will enter credit card payment information.

5. The customer will select Submit.

6. The system will verify the information, save the order as pending, and forward payment information to the accounting system.

7. When payment is confirmed, the order is marked confirmed, an order ID is returned to the customer, and the use case ends.

Alternative Paths

At any time before selecting submit, the customer can select Cancel. The order is not saved and the use case ends.

In step 7, if any information is incorrect, the system will prompt the customer to correct the information.

Place Order use case, the customer can cancel the order at any time before it is submitted.

So, when the use case is executing, if the user selects Cancel, we jump to the alternative flow of events and execute it. This technique can be applied to exception handling as well as interrupt handling in use cases.

HANDLING COMPLEX USE CASES

The Place Order use case is relatively detailed but is still not complete. We haven't considered all possible error conditions, for example, nor have we really detailed the interaction with the customer or customer rep. The system may behave somewhat differently for each of these actors. What about access control and logon permissions? This is a relatively simple use case. How can we handle the more complex use cases?

A complete use case description can get quite complicated. This is not something you write at the very beginning. This is a description that evolves over time. Instead of trying to write everything at once, we will break the task into logical pieces, writing a small part of the use case at a time.

We will start writing the basic path by choosing the most common sequence of steps for the use case flow of events. This is called the *primary scenario* of the use case. After writing the primary scenario, we can add alternatives to the flow of events using branching and alternative flows. Or, we can write the alternatives as separate flows of events. These separate flows are the *secondary scenarios* of the use case.

SCENARIOS

If you pick one particular path through the use case, that is called a scenario. For the Place Order use case just described, some of the scenarios include:

- An order arrives that is complete, with the correct payment.
- An order arrives that is missing a payment.
- An order arrives that is missing a shipping address.

Each of these scenarios describes one path through the Place Order use case. If you combine all the scenarios for Place Order, you get the complete use case. Each scenario represents one instance of the use case.

There are several different ways to document the complete use case: write a complete description in one place as in the example at the beginning of the chapter, let the use case name be a chapter heading in a book with each section in the chapter describing one of the scenarios for that use case, or write out a basic description for the use case with each scenario telling how it differs from the basic description.

No matter which way you choose to document the use case, you can tackle the problem of writing a complete use case description by identifying and describing the scenarios for a use case. We will consider the scenarios in two parts. The primary scenario will describe the basic functionality of the use case. There is one primary scenario for each use case. The secondary scenarios describe alternatives and error conditions for the use case.

This chapter will deal with writing a primary scenario for each use case. The next chapter goes into secondary scenarios in more detail.

THE PRIMARY SCENARIO

The primary scenario is written as if everything goes right. There are no bugs, no errors; it is a perfect world. It is often called the happy day scenario. There must be one primary scenario for each use case.

Scenarios are written from the actor's point of view. Each scenario is a sequence of events that describes the functionality of the use case. You also can think of it as a list of steps to go through to accomplish the use case.

Start a scenario by indicating who begins the scenario and what they are doing. Continue listing steps and finish by indicating how the scenario ends. Scenarios are a series of simple declarative statements with no branching or alternatives.

As you go through this process, you may find new pieces of your architecture, new actors for your system, or new risk factors for the project. Update all your documents to reflect what you learn as you write the scenarios.

"Hi," Gus murmured as he sat down. "Sorry I'm late. I got stuck at work. Where are we?"

"We're looking over the actors for anything we've missed. If you're hungry, Dennis made us save some of his BBQ specialties for you."

"Great! I am starved! Okay, you fill me in while I grab some of that delicious-looking food."

"Well," Tara said, "We were just deciding that we had found all of our actors and use cases but don't know where to go next. We can't figure out how to turn all this stuff into something useful. They show us *what* they work with but not how to turn that information into something we need. For example, how does an order get to shipping?"

"Well, that's what we have to do next. Have you got your list of actors? Good! This is where we put our actors to work, and see how the system flows. What

Exhibit 3-6 Place Order Primary Scenario

> **Flow of Events:**
> *Primary Scenario*
> 1. The use case starts when the customer selects Place Order.
> 2. The customer enters his or her name and address.
> 3. The customer will enter product codes for the desired products.
> 4. The system will supply a product description and price for each item.
> 5. The system will keep a running total of items ordered as they are entered.
> 6. The customer will enter credit card payment information.
> 7. The customer will select Submit.
> 8. The system will verify the information, save the order as pending, and forward payment information to the accounting system.
> 9. When payment is confirmed, the order is marked confirmed, an order ID is returned to the customer, and the use case ends.

we want to do is take each action an actor can do and follow it through our system, one step at a time. Let's look at a customer entering an order." [See Exhibit 3-6.]

"Well," Dennis said, "that was useful. So far, we've found out that we need Place Order to talk to the accounting system, and since Place Order needs a product description and price, it probably also talks to the inventory system."

"Does that mean we have to go back and add it to our use case diagram?"

"Of course! That's exactly what it means. Remember, the diagram was just what we knew about the process at the *exact* time we wrote it down. Now that we have learned more about it, we go back and change it. This way, it grows along with our knowledge."

"Hey, does that mean we have to go back and look at everything else we've done? Like the list of risks, use case diagrams, and so on?"

"Very good, Tara! Yes, it does. As we learn more about our system, we update all documentation to match what we learned. Let's finish writing a primary scenario for each use case, then go back and update our diagrams to match what we learn."

"Well," Gus said, "this diagram [Exhibits 3-7a and 3-7b] is getting rather messy. There are some techniques for cleaning it up. But let's review our primary scenarios first, then come back to this diagram and clean it up."

Exhibit 3-7a   Order-Processing Use Cases

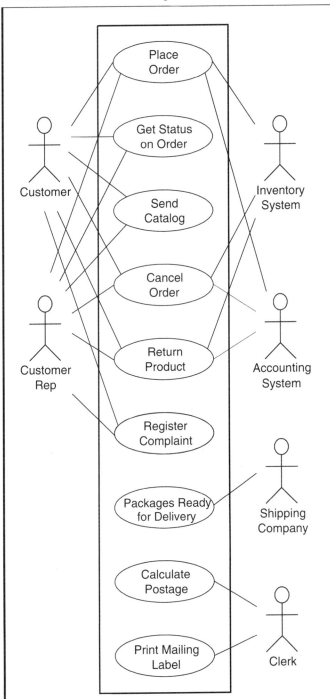

Exhibit 3-7b Order-Processing Use Cases

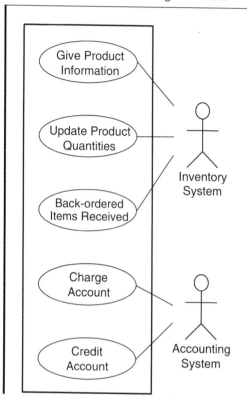

GUIDELINES FOR CORRECTNESS AND COMPLETENESS

Each step of the scenario should be a simple, declarative statement. By default the steps will be in order by time. What if the steps can happen in any order? If this is the case, make it clear in the description. This could be a simple statement at the beginning of the scenario that the steps can run concurrently. Or you might state that some of the steps can happen in any order.

What if you get to a point where you find alternatives? Neither one is an error or a bug. In this case, write down the most likely sequence for the primary scenario.

"Okay," Lisa told Dennis, "We have Customer Places Order written down. But when do we deposit the money? Do we deposit it when the customer orders or after we ship? And what happens if it's a check, not a credit card payment?"

"But I'd hate to charge someone when they order it. What happens if we have to back-order something? They've already paid for it!"

"Hey! Wait a minute!" Gus demanded. "I said we just wanted to write down the happy day scenario. We only want to find the ones where everything goes right. We'll worry about the ones that don't later on, so don't get bogged down on all the variations. Let's go on with the other major things that can happen."

Resist the temptation to get too detailed. We will add more detail over time. But at this point in the process, we are collecting requirements, not doing detailed analysis or design. On the other hand, the scenario needs to be complete. Be very clear on the start and end points, and make sure the list of steps covers in general everything you need to accomplish the functionality of the use case.

You will find a large percentage of use cases start and end with an actor. From our order-processing system, we see that Place Order starts and ends with the customer. Some smaller number of use cases start with an actor and end internally. The UML does not allow use cases to start from inside the system, but we have found this convenient when dealing with time. For example, if our order-processing system is automated to check once a week and place an order for back-ordered items from a supplier, this would start internally and end with the supplier actor.

By definition, scenarios are written from the actor's point of view. Therefore, all the steps in your scenarios should be visible to or easily surmised by the actor.

Scenarios are a communication tool. They are effective only when they communicate information about how the system works to the reader. It is important to consider who will be reading the scenarios. Will it be end users, marketing specialists, developers, or management? Whoever it is, they have to be able to understand the scenarios. If they don't, then the scenarios need to be rewritten.

Another correctness check is to look at each primary scenario one by one. For each step ask yourself, "What is the most likely thing to occur here?" That is what should be written for that particular step.

Don't worry about getting the scenarios perfect. The nature of the process is to be iterative; you keep looking back over work you have already done and refine it to reflect knowledge learned. The scenarios will improve as your understanding of the system improves.

On the other hand, you must include enough information in the scenarios to be able to determine whether a particular use case handles a particular functionality.

OTHER REQUIREMENTS

As you go through writing a primary scenario for each use case, you may find some requirements for your system that are not visible to the actors. Or you may have some special requirements that are hard to express in use cases. These could be things such as timing and size requirements for real time systems. Or for our order-processing software, we have a requirement to provide fast, efficient service, which doesn't turn into a use case. Instead, it affects a lot of other use cases.

These other requirements need to be written and kept with your use cases. They also are a part of your system. They are things that will have to be included as you build and test the system. You can include them in an Other Requirements document that is kept with the use cases documents. Like the use cases, these requirements can be prioritized and managed by a requirements management tool.

If the requirements are specific to a particular use case, you can add a special requirements section to the use case description (see Exhibit 3-8). For example, we will require the Place Order use case to respond to any user input within one second.

Exhibit 3-8 Special Requirements

Place Order

Precondition: A valid user has logged into the system.

Flow of Events:

Primary Scenario

1. The use case starts when the customer selects Place Order.

2. The customer enters his or her name and address.

3. The customer enters product codes for items he or she wishes to order.

4. The system will supply a product description and price for each item.

5. The system will keep a running total of items ordered as they are entered.

6. The customer enters credit card payment information.

7. The customer selects Submit.

8. The system will verify the information, save the order as pending, and forward payment information to the accounting system.

9. When payment is confirmed, the order is marked confirmed, an order ID is returned to the customer, and the use case ends.

Postcondition: The order has been saved in the system marked confirmed.

Special Requirements:

The system must always respond to user input within one second.

PRESENTATION STYLES

Scenarios can be written very formally or in a less formal style. Keep in mind who will be reading the scenarios and choose a style that is comfortable for the readers. Potential readers of scenarios include end users, customers, marketing specialists, customer advisory boards, users groups, testers, technical writers, system architects, system engineers, several levels of management, and developers.

A scenario could be written as informal text (see Exhibit 3-9). Or it could be a numbered list of steps as shown in Exhibit 3-10. Or it could be pseudocode as shown in Exhibit 3-11.

Choose a style that is best for your intended audience. Our experience is that, in general, a numbered list is easier to understand across a wider range

Exhibit 3-9 Informal Text Form of Use Case

Cancel Order Primary Scenario

When the customer rep receives a request to cancel an order, the customer rep finds the order in the system and marks it canceled. Then a request is sent to the accounting system to credit the customer's account.

Exhibit 3-10 Numbered Steps Form of Use Case

Cancel Order Primary Scenario

1. The use case begins when the customer rep receives a request to cancel an order.
2. The customer rep enters an order ID.
3. The customer rep presses Find.
4. The system will display that order.
5. The system marks the order canceled.
6. The accounting system is notified to credit the customer's account and the use case ends.

Exhibit 3-11 Pseudocode Form of Use Case

```
Cancel Order Primary Scenario
Order = CustomerService.CancelOrder(OrderNumber)
   Order.Status = canceled
   Accounting.SendRefund(Customer, Order.Amount)
```

of audience types. It shows each step distinctly, steps can be referred to by number in discussions, and it is an easy style to read for most audiences.

CHAPTER REVIEW

In this chapter, we have looked at the basic form of a use case, which includes precondition, flow of events, and postcondition. We created the first flow of events for each use case by writing one primary scenario. Then we reviewed it for correctness and completeness. Table 3-1 shows the deliverables that should be complete.

We also considered different styles for writing scenarios, each appropriate for a different kind of audience. The next chapter continues with detailing the secondary scenarios for each use case.

Table 3-1 Elaboration Phase Deliverables

Complete	Deliverables
✔	Detailed primary scenarios
	Secondary scenarios
	Activity diagrams
	User interface diagrammed (optional)
	Architecture
	Project plan

Chapter 4

Secondary Scenarios

In Chapter 3 we looked at describing the basic functionality of the use case with the primary scenario. To completely define a use case, you need to identify scenarios for alternate paths and scenarios for error conditions. These can be added to the basic path or written as secondary scenarios. Writing secondary scenarios will work the same as writing primary scenarios. But now we are dealing with errors and alternatives to the primary scenario.

"Okay Gus," Tara called, "We've got a primary scenario for each and every use case that we wrote up. I think I see how this is starting to help us! Now what?"

"Well, now we keep going. Remember back awhile ago, when you tried to write down a use case where things went wrong? I stopped you then because we wanted to focus on getting down the major pieces. Now that we have them, we go back and fill them out. That is to say, we start with, oh, Customer Places Order. Then we follow it through one step at a time. At each step, we think of all the things that can go wrong."

"Wow!" Lisa exclaimed, "That could be quite a list!"

"Well, we don't want to write down *all* of the possibilities in detail or we'd end up doing our entire project in English. We want to write down representative actions. For example, if we are doing a scenario where the deposited money from a customer order doesn't go into our account. What could be the reasons? Well, they could have closed the account, there could have been insufficient funds, or any number of other reasons. But the main focus for us would be that it didn't go into our account. That's the only one we would document."

"Okay, that sounds a little better. How should we find these? And how do we write them down?"

"One way is to take one of your primary scenarios and then, line by line, ask what can go wrong or what can be done differently. Each time you get a different answer, it's a new scenario. Let's start writing and see what we end up with."

FINDING SECONDARY SCENARIOS

An alternative scenario is one that allows a different sequence of events than what was used for the primary scenario. Maybe a user could pick one of several things to do at some point in the use case. The most likely choice was documented in the primary scenario. Now we document the rest of the choices as alternative scenarios.

An exception scenario is one where we handle errors. What could go wrong and what will we do about it? What if a transaction is cancelled in the middle? What do we do in that situation?

A method for finding secondary scenarios is to go through the primary scenarios line by line and ask questions:

- Is there some other action that can be taken at this point? (an alternative scenario)
- Is there something that could go wrong at this point? (an exception scenario)
- Is there some behavior that could happen at any time? (an alternative scenario unless it is an error, then it would be an exception scenario)

Each secondary scenario needs a name and/or a brief description.

Place Order Secondary Scenarios

Payment not there
Order incomplete
Order gets lost
Customer can't login
Shipping address is incomplete
Product code doesn't match actual products
Product no longer carried
Payment bad
Customer pays by check
Customer sends order by mail
Customer phones in order

That's all you will do for now. For each primary scenario, simply list all the alternative and exception scenarios you can think of. As you identify the alternative and exception scenarios, update the list of assumptions with any new ones you find. The list will be included in the documentation that is reviewed by customers, marketing, users, or whoever is defining your project.

DETAILING SIGNIFICANT BEHAVIOR

Secondary scenarios that are important or complex also will need a sequence of steps detailing their behavior. You can write them the same way you write the primary scenarios. Pick a readable style, check for completeness and correctness, and keep your writing style consistent with the primary scenarios.

"Well," Lisa said, putting down her pen, "I think I'm getting the hang of this. We're just putting names down, not the detailed list of steps like before."

"Right. But some of these we will pick out and write up a detailed list of steps."

"How do we pick the ones to detail?" Tara asked.

"Look for scenarios that look like they would be complex or ones you think could be important. We can look over our risk list and pick out scenarios that address those risks. They would be good choices for detailing."

"Hey Gus!" Dennis said. "How about this one? Payment Bad. That's sure important to me, 'cause I'll go out of business if I don't get paid."

"Sure. Let's look for some more."

Instead of documenting the secondary scenarios separately, you can add the alternatives and exceptions descriptions into the primary scenario, as in the example at the beginning of Chapter 3. Alternatives and exceptions can be added directly into the text of the primary scenario, or put in the alternative paths section of the use case.

Remember that you have two different ways of documenting the flow of events for a use case. One way is to document the flow of events with the alternatives and exceptions included in the basic path or the alternative paths section. The other way to document the flow of events is to write a primary scenario that shows exactly one path through the use case with no branching, then document the alternatives and exceptions in separate secondary scenarios. The method of documentation you pick will depend on the complexity of the use case. Simpler use cases can be documented with the alternatives in place. More complex use cases will be easier to read if scenarios are written separately.

How many secondary scenarios should you write? You could write out a complete sequence of steps for every secondary scenario, but this is unnecessarily time-consuming. In many cases secondary scenarios will vary from the primary scenario and from one another by a very small amount.

Instead of writing out a whole sequence of steps, just note the variation in your brief description of the scenario. Writing a complete set of detailed descriptions takes up time that could be put to use building your system. There is no point in building your whole system in a natural language, such as English. There are no automatic English-to-Java translators!

USE CASE DESCRIPTION REVISITED

As you continue refining the flows of events, you may find commonality in the various use cases that you want to abstract out into a common place. Or you may want to extend a use case without changing the original description. You may find a lot of commonality in some of the actors. To take advantage of commonality in your system, you can apply some techniques.

Do not sacrifice clarity for convenience however. Your goal always should be to produce a clear, easy-to-understand document. The techniques are extends, uses, interfaces, and inheritance.

Extends

Extends are used when you have an optional sequence of events you want to include in a use case. Start by determining what you want to add to the use case, and where in the use case it should be added. For example, in our Place Order use case, we might decide we want to add an option to allow special discounts at certain times of the year on certain products. When we have a sale, we want to get the normal product price, then apply the sale discount to it.

Now, update the use case diagram to include extension points (Exhibit 4-2). An extension point is a place in the use case where extension is allowed. The use case is not required to be extended but if it is, the extension points indicate where the extension(s) may occur. Each extension point has a unique name. These names are shown on the use case diagram.

For example, let's say National Widgets calls us and says we need to add a requirement to offer special discounts to frequent customers, and offer sales on selected merchandise at various times. In the Place Order use case, we have to allow for these special situations. So we'll add an extension point after getting the price for an item, to allow applying a sale price to that item. We'll also add an extension point after getting the order total so we can apply a special customer discount to the whole order. We also can show extension points on the use case diagram by adding an extension point compartment to the use case oval, as shown in Exhibit 4-2. Notice that we did not change the use case description. The use case being extended does not change.

Exhibit 4-1 Place Order Use Case

1. The use case starts when the customer selects Place Order.

2. The customer enters his or her name and address.

3. The customer will enter product codes for the products to be ordered.

4. The system will supply a product description and price for each item.

5. The system will keep a running total of items ordered as they are entered.

6. The customer will enter credit card payment information.

7. The customer will select Submit.

8. The system will verify the information, save the order as pending, and forward payment information to the accounting system.

9. When payment is confirmed, the order is marked confirmed, an order ID is returned to the customer, and the use case ends.

Exhibit 4-2 Place Order Diagram with Extension Points

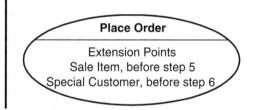

Finally, write a use case describing what will happen at the extension point. The extension includes a conditional expression. When the extension point is reached, if the condition is true, the steps in the extension are executed. The condition will be shown in the text of the extending use case. The extending use case also should indicate which extension point it is using.

Extending Use Case Seasonal Sale Price

**if product in Seasonal Sale list then
At Sale Item Extension**

1. The system will get the sale discount for the product.

2. The system will display the discount on the order.

3. The system will calculate a discount amount by multiplying the original price by the sale discount.

4. The system will subtract the discount amount from the order total.

Extending Use Case Frequent Customer Discount

if customer in Special Customer list then
Special Customer Extension

1. The system will get the customer discount.

2. The system will display the discount on the order.

3. The system will calculate a discount amount by multiplying the order total by the customer discount.

4. The system will subtract the discount amount from the order total.

The relationship between the use case and its extensions is shown on the use case diagram in Exhibit 4-3.

It's important to note that our extended use case, which was Place Order in Exhibit 4-1, must work whether or not it is extended. It cannot know that it has been extended. Extension is allowed but may never take place. In our example, we could choose to never have sales or offer special discounts.

If we have a sale, we will do the Place Order use case as usual, but at the extension point we will add the steps from Seasonal Sale Price. Then we will continue with the steps of Place Order. If we don't have a sale, we do not execute the extension.

More than one use case can extend from the same point. More than one extension can be executed for the same extension point. When the extension point is reached, the conditions in all the extending use cases for that point are evaluated. Every extension with a true condition is executed. The order of execution of the extending use cases is undefined.

Exhibit 4-3 Place Order Diagram with Extending Use Cases

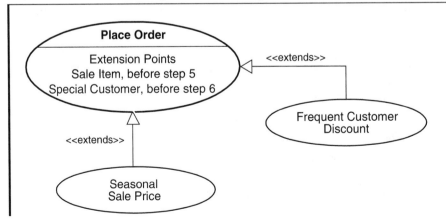

For example, let's add another extending use case for the sale item extension point. If an item is on a seasonal sale and it is overstocked, both of these extending use cases will be executed at the sale item extension point.

Extending Use Case Overstock Product Sale

**if product in Overstock list and amount of product on hand >
maximum stock level then
Sale Item Extension**

1. The system will get the sale discount for the product.
2. They system will display the discount on the order.
3. The system will calculate a discount amount by multiplying the original price by the sale discount.
4. The system will subtract the discount amount from the order total.

We also want to update the use case diagram (see Exhibit 4-4) to include this additional extending use case. The extending use case may include steps for more than one extension point in the use case. The conditional expression is evaluated once when the first extension point is reached. If it is true, then all the steps in the extending use case are inserted at the appropriate extension points.

Exhibit 4-4 Place Order Diagram with Extending Use Cases

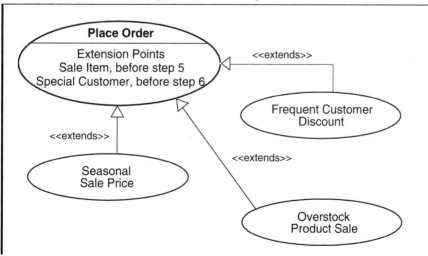

For example, let's say we want to add debugging to our Place Order use case. We want to do something at every extension point in Place Order if debugging is turned on. We can do this with one extending use case. If debugging is turned on, all the steps in this use case will be inserted into Place Order at the appropriate extension points.

Extending Use Case Debugging

if debugging is true then
At Sale Item Extension

1. print "We checked for sale items"

At Special Customer Extension

1. print "We checked for special customers"

Uses

If you find yourself cutting and pasting the same block of text over and over, it indicates you have something generic you can reuse. You can abstract the common behavior with a uses relationship. Start out by identifying the steps that you want to use in many places. Put the steps in a use case and give them a name.

For example, in our order-processing system we need a set of steps to search for an order by customer ID, order ID, or customer name. This searching is done from many of the use cases, including Get Status on Order, Cancel Order, Return Product, and so on. We'll call this use case Find Order.

Find Order Use Case

1. The customer may enter an order ID, customer ID, or customer name.
2. The customer will click on Find.
3. If the customer entered an order ID
   a) the system will display that order.
4. If the customer entered a customer name or customer ID
   a) the system will return a list of all orders for that customer.
   b) The customer will select one order from the list.
   c) The system will display that order.

Now, remove these steps from the original use cases and replace them with a reference to the new use case.

Cancel Order Use Case with Uses Relationship

1. The customer requests to cancel an order.
2. **Use Find Order.**
3. If the order status is confirmed
    a) the order is marked canceled.
    b) The accounting system is notified to credit the customer's account.
4. If the order status is shipped
    a) the customer is notified of National Widgets' return policy.

When the Cancel Order use case reaches the Use Find Order step, it executes the steps of Find Order, then returns to Cancel Order and continues with the next step. We also can show this relationship on a use case diagram (see Exhibit 4-5).

It is important to note that the Using use case is no longer complete by itself. It must have the use cases it is using to be complete. On the other hand, the use case being used does not know when or if it is being used. Therefore it cannot have dependencies on any use case that is using it. In our example in Exhibit 4-5, Cancel Order is not a complete use case. It must have Find Order to be complete. But, Find Order does not know that it is being used by Cancel Order.

A use case can use any number of other use cases. You can have as many levels of using as you desire. From our example, Find Order itself could use other use cases. Or, Cancel Order could be used by other use cases.

Exhibit 4-5 Cancel Order Diagram with Used Use Case

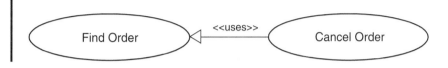

Inheritance

In the use case diagram, inheritance can be used between actors. There is no inheritance between use cases. Inheritance between actors means that one actor fills the same roles as another actor. It also may fill additional roles. It

Exhibit 4-6 Example of Inheritance Between Actors

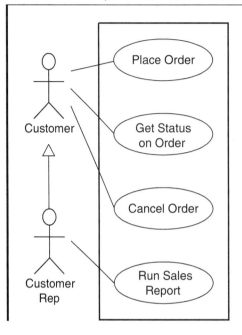

interacts with the same uses cases in the same way. In the UML, inheritance is indicated by a generalization relationship.

Let's look at a simple example from the order-processing system. Customer and Customer Rep have the same set of use cases they interact with. We can clean up the diagram (Exhibit 4-6) a lot by putting inheritance between these actors. We'll present only a couple of the use cases for now to show the notation.

In this example, Customer interacts with the use cases Place Order, Get Status on Order, and Cancel Order. Customer Rep also interacts with Place Order, Get Status on Order, and Cancel Order. Since it inherits from Customer, it inherits all the relationships Customer has to these use cases. In addition, Customer Rep interacts with the use case Run Sales Report. The customer is not allowed to do this.

Interfaces

Interfaces can be defined for actors, use cases, or both. An interface tells what we expect the entity to do. The interface is not part of the actor or the use case; rather, it is a description of how to interact with the actor or use case. You can have more than one interface for any actor or use case.

So start out by defining the interface. An interface has a name and a set of operation signatures. An operation signature tells us what kind of data is passed with the operation and what kind of data is returned when the operation is complete. The operation tells what we expect the entity to do. If we go through the Place Order primary scenario, we can expect the following behavior from the Place Order use case and from the customer actor.

Interface Example for Place Order Use Case

```
Place Order()
Get Product Description and Price(Product ID)
   return Description, Price
Add Price to Total(Price) return Total
Submit Order() return Order ID
```

Interface Example for Customer Actor Use Case

```
Enter Name and Address() return Name, Address
Enter Product Code() return Product Code
Enter Credit Card Information() return Card Number, Expiration Date
```

The customer actor interacts with a number of use cases. We could put all the behavior in the customer interface. Or we could define separate interfaces for the different kinds of behavior we expect from Customer. If we look at Cancel Order, we see there is additional behavior for our customer—searching for an order. We could define a new interface for this behavior.

Adding a Separate Order Search Interface

```
Enter Order ID() return Order ID
Enter Customer Name() return Customer Name
Enter Customer ID() return Customer ID
```

Or we could add the behavior to the existing interface.

Expanding One User Interface

```
Enter Name and Address() return Name, Address
Enter Product Code() return Product Code
Enter Credit Card Information() return Card Number, Expiration Date
Enter Order ID() return Order ID
Enter Customer Name() return Customer Name
Enter Customer ID() return Customer ID
```

We favor using a larger number of small interfaces. This makes the system more flexible to change in future. An entire interface can be added or removed easily, rather than changing an existing interface. You also may want to use the same interface with more than one actor or use case. Keeping the interface small makes it more reusable. So we would add the extra interface for Cancel Order rather than putting it in with user interface.

Now that we have defined the interfaces, we want to add them to the use case diagram (Exhibit 4-7). The straight line between the entity and the interface means the entity supports the interface. The dashed arrow indicates who uses the interface. The use case itself does not use the interface. We will see later in the book that use cases are implemented by classes. The classes that implement the use case will use the interface on the actor. So actors associate with use cases, actors and use cases support interfaces, and classes implement and use the interfaces.

If our actor is not a person, the interface will be the exact programmatic commands we use to interface with that actor. For example, if the actor is a network, the interface might be TCP/IP commands. If the actor is the accounting system that our order-processing software interfaces with, we need to find out what commands can be sent to the accounting system software. Those commands will define the interface to the accounting system actor. For our purposes, we probably will only use a subset of all the possible commands that the accounting system can receive. So our interface will only define the subset that we need.

Exhibit 4-7 Example of Interfaces

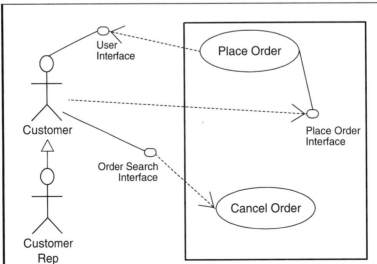

What about our Customer Rep actor? Since it inherits from Customer, it is required to support the interfaces that Customer supports. So the customer rep actor will have the behavior defined by the user interface and the order search interface.

Actors and use cases with interfaces have to support the behavior of the interface. We don't care how the behavior is implemented, as long as it conforms to the interface we have defined. So for example, my customer has to be able to enter a name and address and return them to the system. I don't care how the customer does this. He or she could have a form on a computer or a voice-activated system, or use the buttons on a telephone. As long as my order-processing system gets a name and address, it doesn't care how the information is entered.

Since Customer Rep is a different actor from Customer, it could choose to implement the interfaces differently. I might implement the user interface for Customer using computer forms, but implement the user interface for Customer Rep using a voice-activated system. This is a benefit of defining two different actors, even though they interact with the same set of use cases. You could use this mechanism to support different levels of access to the system. So when the customer logs on, the implementation of the interfaces might restrict his or her access to the system. When the customer rep logs on, the implementation of the same interfaces will be different and will allow access to more of the system.

Let's take the use case diagram for National Widgets from Chapter 3 (Exhibits 3-7*a* and 3-7*b*) and apply these techniques to make the diagram easier to read.

"Hey Gus," Lisa said, "You promised to show us how to make our use case diagram less messy. Can we do it now?"

"Yes, it's really starting to bug me," Tara chimed in.

"Okay," Gus replied. "We'll add in inheritance between our customer and customer rep actors to get rid of a bunch of the lines."

"Well, that's a good starting point," Dennis said after the changes had been made. "But from our use case documents, it looks like Update Product Quantities really is part of a lot of our use cases. Shouldn't that be broken out and made into a uses relationship?"

"You're right. And there are some other uses relationships too," Gus said. "Let's look over all our descriptions and update the diagram to match." [See Exhibits 4-8*a* and 4-8*b*.]

Exhibit 4-8a Order-Processing Use Cases

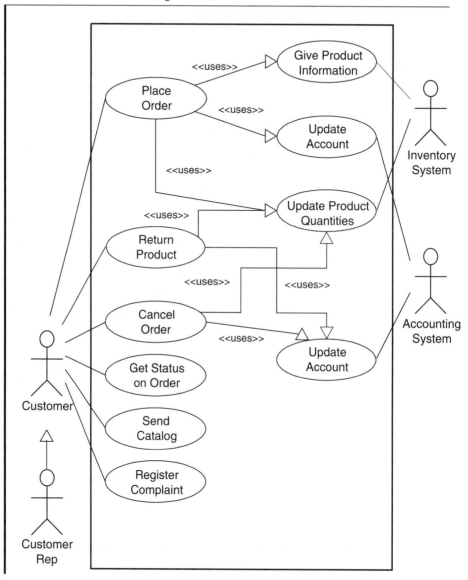

Exhibit 4-8*b*   Order-Processing Use Cases

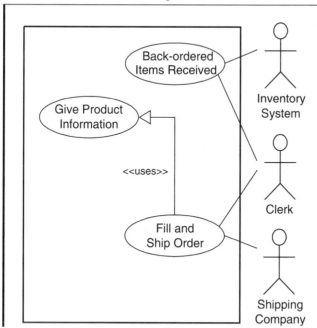

CHAPTER REVIEW

Secondary scenarios are the alternatives and exceptions to the primary scenario of a use case. Everything discussed in this chapter could be applied directly to the primary scenario. In this manner the primary scenario becomes the complete use case flow of events over time.

On the other hand, you may choose to keep the secondary scenarios separate from the primary scenario. This is the best choice for complex use cases.

Use extends, uses, inheritance, and interfaces to add clarity to your documentation and diagrams. After applying these techniques, the goal is to end up with easier-to-read documentation that more closely matches how things are really done, or how you want them to be done. You won't use all of these techniques all the time. And, you won't use them when you first start defining use cases. Like our example problem, you will get the basic use case and relationships defined first, then you will apply some of these techniques to add information or make the documentation easier to understand.

Elaboration phase deliverables completed so far are shown in Table 4-1. Sometimes a written description of a use case or scenario can be hard to

Table 4-1 Elaboration Phase Deliverables

Complete	Deliverables
✔	Detailed primary scenarios
✔	Secondary scenarios
	Activity diagrams
	User interface diagrammed (optional)
	Architecture
	Project plan

understand. This is especially true when you have a lot of branching or exceptions. In the next chapter we'll look at a simple way to diagram the steps of a use case. The diagrams can be used in place of the text or to supplement the text descriptions.

Chapter 5

Diagramming Use Cases

We have spent a lot of time writing text for our use cases. But, as the old saying goes, a picture is worth a thousand words. In this chapter we'll look at two kinds of "pictures" we can use to add detail to, or clarify, our use cases. We'll use activity diagrams to document the steps of the use case. We'll use storyboarding to show the sequence of events from the user interface point of view. These pictures we create can be used with the text descriptions or in place of the text descriptions. Let clarity and good communication guide your choice of techniques.

ACTIVITY DIAGRAMS

Activity diagrams have been used in many forms under many different names over the last few decades. The UML defines an activity diagram as "a subset of a state diagram where the states are all action states and the transitions are automatic." This sounds complicated, but the diagrams actually are very easy to use and read. They can be safely shared with customers, even those unfamiliar with software engineering. We'll start by looking at a simple activity diagram, then see how to extend it to show branching, repetition, and conditions.

"Hey, Gus," Lisa said, "I'm getting really tired of all this writing. Isn't there some easier way to show what these use cases do?"

"Sure. We can use activity diagrams to show the flow of events of the use case."

"What are activity diagrams, and if they are easier than use cases, why didn't we start with them?"

"Well," Gus said, "I felt we would get farther at the start if we wrote it in English, and there are some abilities, such as uses and extends, that can't be shown in an activity diagram. Let's take our Place Order use case as an example.

Place Order Use Case

1. The use case starts when the customer selects Place Order.
2. The customer enters his or her name and address.
3. The customer will enter product codes for products to be ordered.
4. The system will supply a product description and price for each item.
5. The system will keep a running total of items ordered as they are entered.
6. The customer will enter credit card payment information.
7. The customer will select Submit.
8. The system will verify the information, save the order as pending, and forward payment information to the accounting system.
9. When payment is confirmed, the order is marked confirmed, an order id is returned to the customer, and the use case ends.

Gus continued, "Each activity in the use case will be represented by a rounded rectangle on a diagram. Transitions from one activity to another are represented by arrows." [See Exhibit 5-1.]

"Well, that looks okay, but it seems like some things are missing," Tara mused.

"Yeah," Dennis chimed in. "Don't we want to let customers order more than one product? And how can we show that we want to mark the order confirmed only if accounting approves?"

"We need to add conditions to our diagram [see Exhibit 5-2], Gus," said Lisa, busily indicating places for conditions. "They go in square brackets, so let's add them where we need them. I think I'll replace the action Select Place Order with a condition so we don't have to go directly to placing an order every time we log in."

"Good idea, Lisa!"

"Okay Lisa," Tara said. "Explain to me what all the new symbols mean."

"Well, the phrases in square brackets are conditions. That means we can take that path only if the condition is true. So after Log In, we can't get to Order Form Displayed until the user selects Place Order. The condition stops us from going down that path until it is true."

"That's what we want." Dennis laughed. "But what about the bullet and the bull's-eye?"

"The bullet is the starting point. The bull's-eye is the stopping point. On our diagram it was pretty clear where to start and stop, but if the diagram gets more complicated, we'll have to show them explicitly."

"That's looking more like it. Hey, Lisa! We have a bunch of different options from log in. Do we show them all the same way?"

Exhibit 5-1 Simple Activity Diagram Example

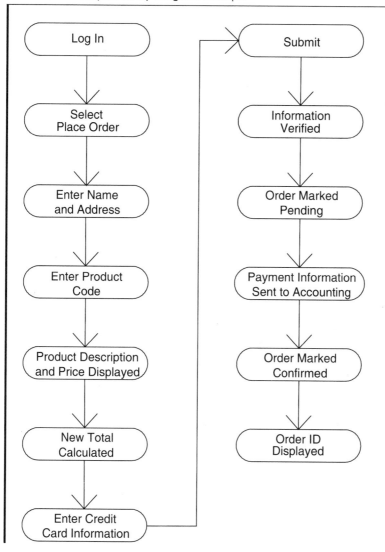

"We could, but I think it would be easier to show a decision point. That way the diagram will show clearly that we have to make a choice at this point. I'll redo part of the diagram so you can see it. We can use the decision point anywhere we have a decision to make. It's represented by a diamond." [See Exhibit 5-3.]

"Can we have only two arrows coming out of the diamond?"

"No. You can have as many arrows as you want coming out of the diamond, but they all have to be labeled with conditions. You also can have as many arrows as you want coming into the diamond."

Exhibit 5-2 Activity Diagram—Conditional Example

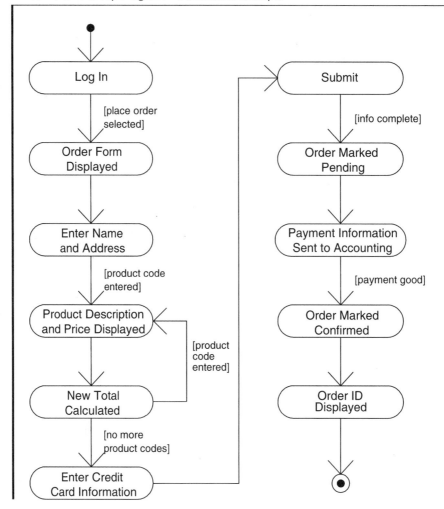

"I like these diagrams. I think it will be easier to show our alternatives for error handling or multiple decision points in this diagram rather than in text. Let's try some more use cases."

So far, everything we've shown allows for only one thread of activity. What if you want to allow multiple, parallel activities? Say, for example, that we only allow a customer to bring up one screen at a time. But when a customer rep logs in, we want all the different kinds of screens to come up at once, so when a customer calls, the rep doesn't have to wait while a screen is displayed. With the decision point we just discussed, we have to pick one choice. Exhibit 5-4 shows the diagram drawn with something called a fork.

Exhibit 5-3 Activity Diagram—Decision Point Example

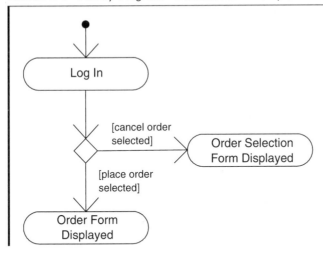

Exhibit 5-4 Activity Diagram—Fork Example

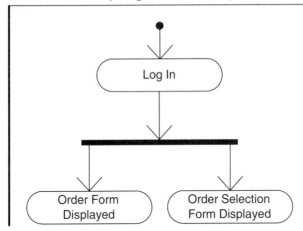

The heavy line is the fork point. At this point the single path from Log In divides into two parallel paths. We are now allowing the order form and the order selection form to be displayed at the same time. Why is it called a fork instead of something like a separation or a divide? Think of a table fork with one handle that divides into multiple tines. The fork diagram in Exhibit 5-3 looks a little like a table fork. You can have as many paths coming out of the fork as you would like. There is only one path coming into the fork.

Similarly, we can show when multiple paths join back together. This is actually called a *join*. It looks like the fork, except we will have multiple paths coming into the join and one path coming out of the join. Let's assume that all the screens for the customer rep have to be closed before the rep can log off.

Exhibit 5-5 Activity Diagram—Join Example

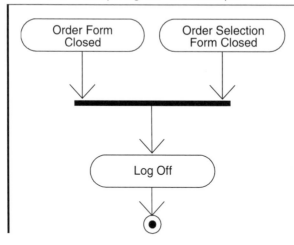

In Exhibit 5-5, we will not get to Log Off until both screens have closed. We wait at the join point until all the paths coming into the join have arrived, then we continue.

What we've shown in these activity diagrams is a subset of what is possible. This much will allow you to diagram the use cases. The things we can add to this diagram later include objects that handle the activities on the diagram, subsystems that handle the activities on the diagram, and message and signal passing. Because we aren't working with any of those things right now, we won't go into that notation.

If you find that the diagram is getting really large and complex, split it into pieces. The rounded rectangle representing the activity actually could take the place of a whole diagram.

In Exhibit 5-6, Cancel Order Process could be another complete activity diagram showing the events for canceling an order. This way, we can see its relationship to logging in and that it is one of several options without having to put all the details in this diagram.

DIAGRAMMING THE USER INTERFACE

In some projects the user interface is critical to the project. For example, let's suppose National Widgets is going to do all their business through the Web. In such a case, you should diagram the user interface early in the process. This sample of the user interface can be shared with potential users early in the project in order to find any serious problems with it. You also may find new requirements, such as restricting who can log into the system. It can also help

Exhibit 5-6 Activity Diagram—Referencing Other Diagrams Example

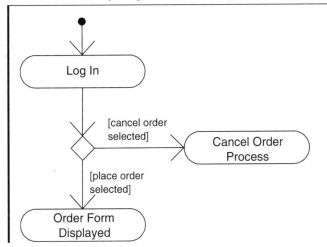

your team clarify issues or problems found when trying to write or diagram the flow of events.

The user interface could be diagrammed in the form of a storyboard. A storyboard is a series of drawings. The first drawing shows what the user interface looks like at the start. Each time there is a significant change to the look of the interface, a new drawing is made showing the updated interface.

"Hey, Gus."

"Yes, Dennis?"

"I'm not a real abstract thinker, so I'm really getting confused trying to figure out what the user is doing in front of the screen. Do you have a nifty diagram someone like me can use to see what the user interface is like?"

"I do have an idea for you, Dennis. It comes out of the movie industry and is called storyboarding. What we'll do is draw pictures of the user interface at key points in the process."

"How do I know what the key points are?"

"Any time there is a significant change to the user interface, we'll do a new picture. Let's use our typical example of placing an order and storyboard it so you can see if you like the technique." [See Exhibits 5-7, 5-8, and 5-9.]

"Hey wait," Tara exclaimed. "How does our customer know what to order? Does he have a catalog in his hands? What if he wants to look at it online? I think we need another selection on the first screen after login to look at the catalog."

"Can we make people enter a name and address first, before they can do anything else?" Dennis asked. "That way they can't forget to put in that information once they have ordered."

Exhibit 5-7   Storyboard Example 1—First Screen Our User Will See

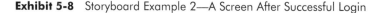

Welcome to National Widgets On-Line Catalog

**Please Enter Your User Name and Password
to Access Our Electronic Catalog**

User Name:

Password:

Exhibit 5-8   Storyboard Example 2—A Screen After Successful Login

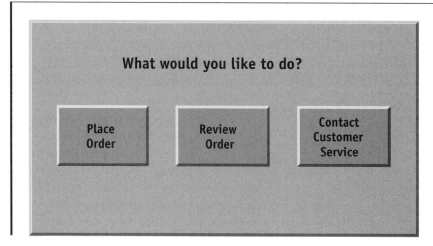

What would you like to do?

**Place
Order**

**Review
Order**

**Contact
Customer
Service**

"Well, I think we should allow people to pick products right out of the catalog and have the order form filled in automatically."

"What about storing things like customer name, address, and credit card info, so frequent customers don't have to enter it all the time?"

"See how many ideas we have come up with just from looking at this one sequence?" Gus asked. "Now we need to look at those ideas to see if they are feasible and if we want to include them in our first order-processing system.

Exhibit 5-9 Storyboard Example 3—A Screen After Selecting Place Order

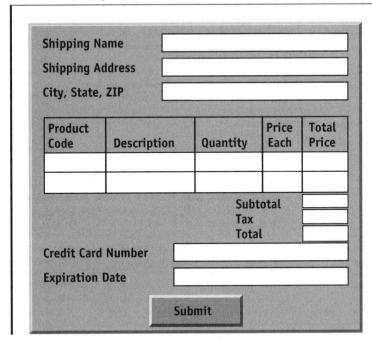

Maybe some of them will be later improvements. Even though they all are good ideas, we may not be able to do everything we would like in the first release of our product."

A storyboard will give your users a good idea of how the user interface works. This will allow your users to give you feedback on what they like or don't like. The storyboard is not designed to show the users a particular look and feel, but rather to see how well the events in a use case flow from a user perspective. It also will help you find alternatives that may not have been obvious from the written text.

Using a software tool to design the user screens as they actually will appear is appealing because users can try out the interface directly on the computer. This can be a fairly quick process, but there is a danger that the users will not understand there is no functionality behind the screens. The system isn't really placing orders, it just looks like it because the screens are all complete. The danger is that your customers or users will think the system is already built. Set their expectations appropriately before letting them use actual screens.

CHAPTER REVIEW

Using activity diagrams to depict use cases sometimes can lead to more clarity than trying to describe the same thing in text. Or you may like using text for the use cases but decide to supplement the text with a few activity diagrams for key parts of the process.

You also may find it useful to storyboard the user interface to help clarify what is happening from the user's point of view. Or you may need to design the user interface early to get acceptance from customers or end users. Using a storyboard lets the user test the flow without being bound to a particular tool, or look and feel standard.

Using software tools to design the user interface is quick and allows end users to try the actual screens as they will appear in the application. The danger is that the user will think the system is complete when all you really have is a bunch of pretty screens. Table 5-1 shows what should be complete now.

In the next chapter we will look at mechanisms for taking projects that are large and complex and breaking them into smaller pieces that are easier to work with.

Table 5-1 Elaboration Phase Deliverables

Complete	Deliverables
✔	Detailed primary scenarios
✔	Secondary scenarios
✔	Activity diagrams
✔	User interface diagrammed (optional)
	Architecture
	Project plan

Chapter 6

Dividing Large Systems

What if you have been going through the process and you keep saying, We need more detail. Everything is too high level, too abstract, and so on? It may be your use cases are not detailed enough. But it's also possible that your system is too big to deal with all together. You need an approach to break the system into pieces until each piece is small enough to work with.

We will start by defining the modules of the architecture of the system. An architecture is specific to a particular application, but we'll go through a few basic architectural patterns in this chapter to give some ideas. These patterns give a basic framework for the system without going into details about the contents of the system. You may find that several of the patterns could be applied to your project. Since software architecture is beyond the scope of this book, we have listed some good books on software architecture in Resources (Appendix A).

After considering architectures, we'll look at how to divide the use cases between the modules of the architecture. We have to consider what to do about actors and how to trace from a high-level system use case to its parts in the various modules of the system.

ARCHITECTURAL PATTERNS

While reading the previous chapters, you may have found yourself identifying significant parts of your system. Or you may have a requirement to develop your system as a three-tier architecture. Or you know your system must be distributed. You would like to capture that information somewhere. The first step will be to consider various patterns of architectures and pick one that looks like it fits your system. You would then go on to add details to the pattern, such as contents of the modules, and interfaces between the modules. As you fill in the details, it will become clearer whether it actually is a fit or not.

An architectural pattern is a generalized overview of the structure of some set of systems. Each pattern is very general so that it applies to a broad range of systems. Looking over some architectural patterns will give you more viewpoints into the problem you are trying to solve. It also may be useful in determining the feasibility of one or more parts of the system being developed.

Start by picking out the major pieces of your system. These should be things that jump out at you as being part of the system. We will present an example for the order-processing software that uses a piece that handles order taking, a piece that processes payments, and a piece that handles shipping the orders. These pieces are represented by UML subsystems.

Next, write descriptions of your subsystems. This will help you determine whether the subsystems are well defined and will help find the interfaces between the subsystems. Which subsystems work with which other subsystems? Finally, as you determine the patterns of relationships, you will want to try matching your subsystems and relationships to some architectural patterns.

We'll look at several architectural patterns here as examples, then examine the process in more detail for the order-processing software. See Appendix A for books on software architecture and architectural patterns.

Three-Tier Architectural Pattern

We will start by looking at a simple three-tier architectural pattern. In this pattern, one tier holds the user interface, one holds the business rules, and one holds the database. Exhibit 6-1 graphs this using subsystem packages from the UML notation. The arrows show a dependency relationship. So, for Business Rules to do its job, it needs something from database.

Where do the pieces of the order-processing software fit in? Each one will be split between the tiers. For example, look at order taking. The form used to

Exhibit 6-1 A Three-Tier Architecture Example

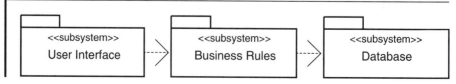

record the order will be a part of the User Interface tier. The data collected for the order will be in the Database tier. The process used for taking an order will be in the Business Rules tier. The other parts will be similarly divided.

This kind of approach could be good if the goals of your system include having a consistent look across all functions, having one database used by everyone, and having a consistent set of business processes. Or possibly, National Widgets decides to start out by buying an order-processing system that is structured as a user interface, business processes, and database. All they need to do then is modify the pieces of this software to fit their particular needs.

Pipe and Filter Architectural Pattern

A very different type of pattern is the pipe and filter. The basic idea of a pipe and filter pattern is that one piece inputs some data, transforms it somehow, and outputs the transformed data. The next piece then takes the information, transforms it somehow, and outputs the transformed data, and so on. Each piece is independent and doesn't know about the other pieces.

What might this look like for our order-processing system? As shown in Exhibit 6-2, Take Orders would do its function, then put a stack of orders somewhere. Ship Orders would pick up a stack of orders, fill, and ship them. Similarly, Process Payments would pick up any payments and process them. The graph of this pattern is different from the three-tier. Note that there are no dependency arrows between our subsystems. Each subsystem does its job completely independent of the others.

We can add and replace subsystems without changing the other subsystems. The only dependency is on the data. We are showing the data here as a subsystem to illustrate the concept. The data might come from standard input and go to standard output. That would be the model for a traditional

Exhibit 6-2 Pipe and Filter Architecture Example

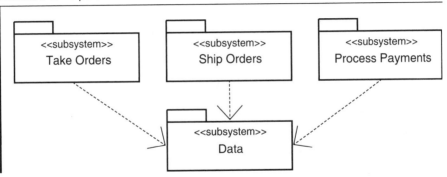

pipe and filter architecture, where the data is piped from one subsystem to another. Each subsystem reads data from standard input, filters, or transforms, the data it receives, and writes the data to standard output. Instead, the data could come from a file or database before it is transformed and written back out.

Pipe and filter is a good approach when you want the flexibility to add and delete subsystems at any time without having to change the other subsystems. Since the only dependency is on the data, it's easy to change a system when the change is adding or removing functionality.

Object-Oriented Architectural Pattern

For the last example (Exhibit 6-3), we'll look at an object-oriented pattern. In this pattern, subsystems are defined around data and its associated functions. The relationships are more flexible than in the other two patterns. Once identified, the subsystems can interrelate any way they need to accomplish the work of the system. In this example, Take Orders has dependencies on Ship Orders and Process Payments, but those subsystems don't know about each other. Take Orders contains orders and the functions that manipulate them. Process Payments deals with charges, credits, and accounts, and Ship Orders deals with packages and shipping information.

This approach emphasizes the dependencies between the pieces of the system, while showing each function as a self-contained separate piece. In contrast, in three-tier architecture, each function exists in three places—part of the function in the user interface, part in business rules, and part in the database. In the pipe and filter architecture, the functions can relate only through the data.

Exhibit 6-3 Object-Oriented Architecture Example

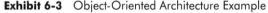

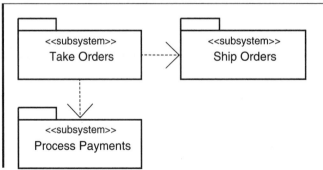

Order-Processing Architecture Example

"Okay, Gus," Tara said, "Now that we have written down everything, we've found out a lot about our system. But we still don't have a good idea on how to turn this into something real! You explained about different types of architecture, but how do we know which one is right?"

"Well, now we take what we can pull out of these lists and draw up our first attempt at an architecture for the order processing software. Let's see. . . . Customers will submit orders, which we then fill and ship to them. Sounds like we need something for order input and also for shipping. And we have to have some way of processing payments. Okay, Let's put these into a chart" [Exhibit 6-4].

"Okay so far. But now we need to figure out how the pieces relate to each other."

"I think they are pretty independent," Lisa said. "One part just enters orders into the system. At another point in time, an order can have its payment information verified. Then later, someone else could pull the order together and ship it."

"I see. So the only relationship so far between the parts is the orders themselves."

"Sounds kind of like it could be, oh, what was that called, Gus? The pipe and filter? Except I'd store the orders in a database somewhere rather than just pass them from part to part."

"Wait a minute," Dennis said. "We've been processing credit card payments as part of taking orders. Wouldn't that add a call between Take Orders and Process Payments?"

"We have to look at this more carefully because we have an inconsistency between our architecture and our process. Does that mean we have the wrong subsystems, the wrong architecture, or the wrong process? We have to change one of them, but what is the best change?"

"I like having all the payment processing stuff together," Lisa said. "No matter what kind of payment—credit card, check, money order—there will be similar things to do, so it makes sense to put them all together."

Exhibit 6-4 Order-Processing Subsystems

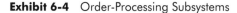
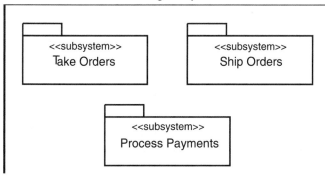

"I think I agree. The Process Payments subsystem seems reasonable. I don't want to split it up."

"What about including it inside Take Order?"

"No, because we need Return Product to do money-type things too."

"Wait a minute. Where is Return Product? And how will Process Payments issue credits?"

"Hold it!" Gus said, raising his hand. "Maybe our names are wrong. What if Process Payments is called Money Handling? Then it can have all the stuff about interfacing to the accounting system, updating accounts, charging and crediting customers, handling checks, credit cards, or money orders, and so on."

"Good. I like having the description of the subsystem. It makes it easier to figure out what is best."

"Ship Orders is still good," Tara continued. "That subsystem can interface with the inventory system to find the parts of the order, then generate a mailing label and calculate shipping and handling for the order. All the things that go into actually packaging up and shipping an order."

"Sure. And that is really independent of the rest of the system. We don't really care how we got the order or how many times it may have changed. It can just work off the database."

"So what about Take Orders? Do we need additional subsystems for Return Product and so on, or can we make a more general subsystem that manages the orders themselves?"

"Why not Manage Orders?" Lisa asked. "It will do all the order taking, returning of products, status of orders, and so on. It will write to the database, use information already in the database, and potentially make calls to Money Handling as well." [See Exhibit 6-5.]

"Will Money Handling use the Database?"

"I don't think so," Dennis replied. "I like the way it is interfacing with the order management piece. It makes more sense to me. Let's try it that way for now."

Exhibit 6-5 Order-Processing Subsystems with Relationships

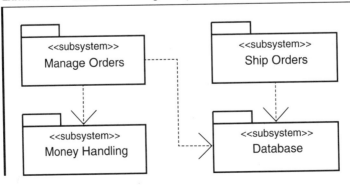

"Hey," Lisa said, "Why aren't we showing our inventory and accounting systems?"

"Actually," Gus added, "since they are actors we don't include them here. This is a diagram of our system and actors are always outside our system."

"It doesn't look like pipe and filter any more."

"No. I think we fixed our problem by changing the architecture and the subsystems and leaving the process alone. It looks more like an object-oriented architecture now."

"Hey, Gus, how do we know we got it right?"

TESTING THE ARCHITECTURE WITH USE CASES

At this point you have identified the basic subsystems for your system, written descriptions for them, identified relationships between them, and identified the basic architectural pattern you are using. But how do you know that what you have is right?

There are a couple of things you can do to test the architecture you have defined to see if it is correct and will basically work for your system. First, apply these module tests to your subsystems to see if they are well defined modules. Each subsystem should have:

- A single functionality
- Strong (internal) cohesion
  - The parts of this subsystem have a strong relationship to each other
- Loose (external) coupling
  - This subsystem doesn't depend much on other subsystems to get its job done
- Minimal communication to other subsystems
  - The subsystems don't do a lot of talking back and forth

Next, take each use case and step through the architecture. For each step of the use case, determine which subsystem will handle that step. If the subsystem has to ask another subsystem to do part of the use case, is there a relationship between the subsystems? Use this process to add to the descriptions of the subsystems, to add relationships between subsystems, to add descriptions to the relationships, and maybe even to add new subsystems. Let's look at the order-processing software for an example.

Gus and his friends have returned from dinner, and continue where they left off.

"Lisa, you asked how we know if we get it right. That's a good question. Anyone?"

"Well," Dennis started, "if we could magically test it somehow. . . ."

"That would be good, yes. Well, I can tell you how we can do some functional testing using the use cases we put together."

"Oh, good!" Tara said. "I was hoping to get more use out of those."

"Here's what we'll do. Let's take a use case," Gus said, ruffling through the use cases stack a bit. "Let's start with Place Order. We'll step through it and assign each step to a subsystem. That will start to tell us who communicates with whom and what they will need to know."

Place Order Step 1

The use case starts when the customer selects Place Order.

Gus started the first one. "Who handles log in and security?"

"It doesn't really fit anywhere currently defined, so I guess we need another subsystem."

"What do we call it?"

"What does it do?"

"It handles log in and log out, and checks for access permissions," responded Lisa. "We don't want customers to have access to our accounting system, for example."

"Well, let's call it System Access then," Gus said. "It will handle step one. Now what?"

Place Order Step 2

The customer enters his or her name and address.

"Sounds like something Manage Orders would do."

"How did we get there?" Gus asked.

Lisa looked puzzled. "What do you mean?" she asked.

"This is one use case. You can't start somewhere and appear somewhere else without going there from where you were. So how did we get there?"

"I guess System Access called Manage Orders to do the order taking."

"So we need an arrow between those subsystems. Next step."

Place Order Step 3

The customer will enter product codes for products he or she wishes to order.

"Manage Orders does this. Next step."

Place Order Step 4

The system will supply a product description and price for each item.

"That sounds like something from the Inventory System."

"But we don't have a subsystem for that because it's an actor."

"Our interface to it is from Ship Orders. Do we want to call Ship Orders to get product information?"

"That doesn't make sense," Tara said. "It's not a shipping function, although Ship Orders needs product information, too."

"Guess we need a subsystem that both Manage Orders and Ship Orders can use," Gus decided. "Let's call it Product Info. We call it to get all kinds of information about products. It can interface with the inventory system, and no one else has to know we are using an inventory system."

"So step four goes to Product Info with an arrow from Manage Orders to Product Info. Got it! Next step."

Place Order Step 5

The system will keep a running total of items ordered as they are entered.

"Manage Orders. Next."

Place Order Step 6

The customer will enter credit card payment information.

"Manage Orders."

"Wait," Dennis said. "Shouldn't it be Money Handling?"

"No. We're just collecting information, not processing the payment."

"Oh, okay, Manage Orders. What's next?"

Place Order Step 7

The customer will select Submit.

"Manage Orders. Next."

Place Order Step 8

The system will verify the information, save the order as pending, and forward payment information to the accounting system.

"Verify Info looks like Manage Orders, but not the rest."

"Yeah. Database should do the save, and payment info goes to Money Handling."

Dennis smiles. "Sounds good to me. And we have those relationships in the diagram [see Exhibit 6-6] already. Next step."

Place Order Step 9

When payment is confirmed, the order is marked confirmed, an order ID is returned to the customer, and the use case ends.

Exhibit 6-6   Order-Processing Subsystems Updated

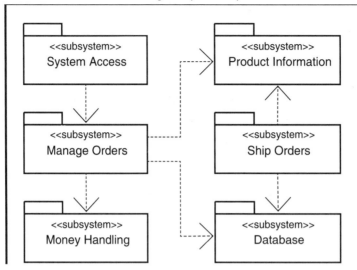

"OK. So we know payment confirmation is Money Handling from the previous step. The rest looks like Manage Orders."

"But we change the status of the order so that it will require the Database to update it."

"Okay. And who generates the order ID?"

"Probably Database because it knows how many are already entered."

"Yeah, but so does Manage Orders, and I think the function fits better there. Database should just be store, retrieve, and update-type functions."

"Hmm. I agree. The order ID can go in Manage Orders. Let's see what we have now, and while we're at it, let's write a description for each subsystem."

System Access Subsystem

This subsystem handles log in and log out, and checks for access permissions.

Product Info Subsystem

This subsystem provides all kinds of information about products. It interfaces with the inventory system.

Manage Orders Subsystem

This subsystem handles order taking, returning of products, status of orders, and canceling orders.

Ship Orders Subsystem

This subsystem prints pick lists for orders, generates mailing labels, and calculates shipping and handling for orders.

Money Handling Subsystem

This subsystem interfaces to the accounting system, updates accounts, charges and credits customers, and handles checks, credit cards, or money orders.

Database Subsystem

This subsystem contains the data we need to store for the application. It provides standard store, retrieve, update, and delete functions for the data that is stored.

DEFINING INTERFACES BETWEEN SUBSYSTEMS

While going through the previous exercise, we found operations that one subsystem called in another subsystem. We drew an arrow to show a relationship existed, but we also need to record what the actual operations are. UML subsystems can include operations in their specification. We have chosen to move the subsystem name into the tab of the package and list the operations of the subsystem in the main compartment of the package. Later, when we have defined classes for the subsystem, we will move those operations to the classes that implement them.

Some of the subsystems don't have operations. Notice that these subsystems are not called by any other subsystem. But, as we go through all the use cases, we may find occasions when we need to make calls to System Access or Ship Orders, or an actor may call those subsystems. If so, we will add operations to those subsystems. The other subsystems have some operations listed in them. For example, under Manage Orders, we show the operations Place Order, Cancel Order, and Return Product because other subsystems expect Manage Orders to supply those operations.

Right now all we have are names. In some cases, we may need to send data to the subsystem along with the operation. For example, in the Database subsystem, in Save Order we send along the order to be saved. Eventually all the operations will be updated to show what data is passed with them, if any. We will continue adding operations to the subsystems as we go through all the use cases in the system.

"Now that we have identified some of the subsystems, let's write out our interfaces with them."

"Wait!" Tara said. "I think I know what you mean. You're telling us to write down what each of these subsystems should be telling the others when they do the work. For example, when we pass a customer order from the Manage Orders subsystem over to the Database subsystem, we have to tell Database which order and what to do with it. That's the definition of the interface, what we tell them as well as the fact that we tell them."

Exhibit 6-7 Order Processing with Operations

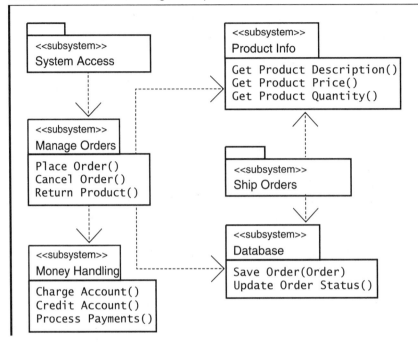

"Exactly! And by writing it down, we solidify our design just a little bit more."

"How do we know our interfaces are complete?"

"We don't right now. The idea here is still to put down what we know now and add to it later as we come across it. Remember? That's how this keeps growing. Every time we learn something new, we add it in, and that tells us more about it."

ALLOCATING USE CASES TO SUBSYSTEMS

Now that we have subsystems defined, we need to divide up the system-level use cases into subsystem-level use cases. We'll do the same sort of process of going through the use cases step by step, but now the purpose is to create new use cases that are subordinates of the system-level use cases.

We already looked at each step of our use cases and allocated them to some subsystem of our architecture. That subsystem is responsible for handling that step. That step becomes a use case for that subsystem. The new use case at the subsystem level is a subordinate use case to the original system-level use case of which it was a step. You also might combine several steps of a system-level use case into one subordinate use case. Or you might end up

Exhibit 6-8   Place Order Superordinate Use Case

1. The use case starts when the customer selects Place Order.

2. The customer enters his or her name and address.

3. The customer will enter product codes for products to be ordered.

4. The system will supply a product description and price for each item.

5. The system will keep a running total of items ordered as they are entered.

6. The customer will enter credit card payment information.

7. The customer will select Submit.

8. The system will verify the information, save the order as pending, and forward payment information to the accounting system.

9. When payment is confirmed, the order is marked confirmed, an order ID is returned to the customer, and the use case ends.

splitting one step from a system-level use case into several subordinate use cases.

Let's look at an example using the Place Order use case. Place Order is a system-level use case for our order-processing software. It is also called a superordinate use case because it has subordinate use cases. Exhibit 6-8 shows the original Place Order use case (see page 26).

Place Order mostly fits within the Manage Orders subsystem. So we'll allocate it to that subsystem and examine the steps to see what doesn't fit in Manage Orders. Those steps will become subordinate use cases in other subsystems. We said Step 1 would be handled by System Access, so it is a subordinate use case of that subsystem. We'll reword it a little to make it more general purpose.

Login Subordinate Use Case

The user logs in to the system and selects an activity from some offered set of activities.

Steps 2 and 3 are handled by the Manage Orders subsystem so we don't need to separate them out. Step 4 is handled by Product Info, so that will go in a separate use case.

Get Product Description and Price Subordinate Use Case

The system will supply a product description and price for each item.

Steps 5 through 7 and verifying information will stay in Manage Orders, so we don't separate them out. In step 8, "save the order as pending" is clearly handled by the Database subsystem.

Save Order Subordinate Use Case

The system will save the order as pending.

The last step also will become more than one subordinate use case. Validating payment information will go to Money Handling, and Update Order Status is another call to the Database subsystem.

Validate Payment Subordinate Use Case

The system will validate the payment.

Update Order Status Subordinate Use Case

The system will update the order status.

Once all the use cases have been distributed, look at the actors for the system. Each of these actors will need to interface with some subsystems in the architecture. Determine with which subsystems to associate the actor. You also will have new actors in your system because each subsystem now becomes an actor to the other subsystems. We will find interactions with the subsystem actors when we add details to the new use cases.

What are the relationships between these subordinate use cases? A use case by definition must execute completely within a module. Uses and extends do not go across module boundaries. This was no problem for our system-level use cases because the whole system was the module. But now our module is one subsystem. The use cases for that subsystem must execute completely within that subsystem. Because the subordinate use cases are in different subsystems and each subsystem is an actor to the others, the relationships between these subordinate use cases will be implemented by communicates associations.

Are there any requirements that were not satisfied by the system-level use cases? These could be internal processes that are not visible to actors at the system level. If you can make one of these internal requirements into a use case, go ahead and do that. Then allocate the new use case to one of your subsystems. You may find you need to add one or more new subsystems to accommodate these internal requirements.

CREATING SUBSYSTEM DOCUMENTATION

At this point, you can treat each subsystem as if it were a whole system. Each one has actors and use cases, so you can create a use case diagram for each subsystem. The new use cases will need descriptions. The whole process as described in this book will be applied iteratively to each subsystem.

Let's look at use case diagrams for a couple of the subsystems we have defined using the new use cases we found for Place Order (Exhibits 6-9 and 6-10). We are adding arrows to the communicates relationship between actor and use case to indicate the direction of communication. So the user starts the Log In use case and sometime in that process, the Log In use case contacts the Manage Orders actor.

Log In Subordinate Use Case
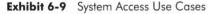

The use case starts when the user starts the log in function.

The user enters a user name and password.

The system verifies the user name and password.

The system sets access levels for the user.

The user selects an activity from a set of choices.

The activity is sent to Manage Orders.

The use case ends.

Exhibit 6-9 System Access Use Cases

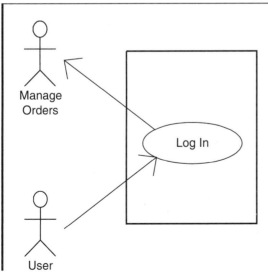

Exhibit 6-10 Manage Orders Use Cases

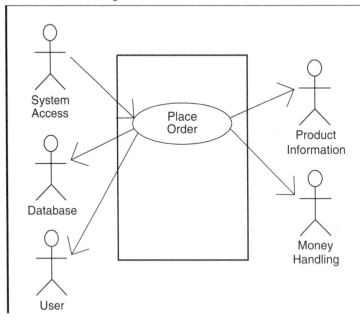

We also want to detail the steps of each of the subordinate use cases as we did for the system-level use cases. This use case can have secondary scenarios, activity diagrams, and a storyboard for the user interface. Each of the new subsystems can have an architecture. So we treat each subsystem as a complete system. You would do similar documentation for all the new subsystems you have defined.

This process can be repeated for as many levels as you need to define your system. Eventually you will reach a point where a subsystem is small enough so that you have enough detail to implement it without further dividing it. If you get to a point where you are calling one class a subsystem, you have gone too far!

CHAPTER REVIEW

In this chapter we have developed what is sometimes called a system of interconnected systems. This is because each subsystem of your system has become a whole system itself. These new systems have interfaces to each other, so they are interconnected. And taken together, they completely describe one higher-level system. We are most of the way through elaboration (see Table 6-1).

Table 6-1 Elaboration Phase Deliverables

Complete	Deliverables
✔	Detailed primary scenarios
✔	Secondary scenarios
✔	Activity diagrams
✔	User interface diagrammed (optional)
✔	Architecture
	Project plan

The next chapter talks about documentation for systems and use cases, and gives some sample templates. In addition, all the currently developed documents for the order-processing system are included.

Chapter 7

Documenting Use Cases

A lot of documentation is associated with use cases and needs to be organized somehow. You want the documentation to be understandable but you need other things as well. For example, you may want to be able to trace from system-level to subordinate use cases, or from use cases to scenarios to test plans. You may want to be able to set priority levels on a use case or any part of a use case and then later run a report listing all use cases of a certain priority. Or you may want to be able to set and check status on a use case, such as whether it has been coded or tested.

In this chapter, we'll look at a sample use case template and consider different methods for implementing that template.

DOCUMENTATION TEMPLATES

What follows are some sample documentation templates. We start with an overall system description (see Exhibit 7-1). You will have just one of these documents. It probably will be in a file or document by itself. We follow that with a document template for a use case.

Next, we need descriptions for the use cases. Each use case most likely will be in a document or file by itself. If a use case has a lot of detailed scenario descriptions, they also might be in separate files. First is a very detailed use case document template (see Exhibit 7-2). You will have one for each system-level use case. You also will have one for each subordinate use case. You will need a similar document for the detailed scenarios. Just leave out the parts that are unnecessary or redundant. These are shown in Appendix B.

Exhibit 7-1 System Description Document Template

System Name
<A brief description. In a large system, this could be several pages. Note this is not meant to be detailed requirements, but a basic overview of the system.>

Risk Factors
<List risk factors here in priority order.>

System-Level Use Case Diagram
<Or you could just list the actors and use cases in text.>

Architecture Diagram
<Include a description of the interfaces as well. These could be on the diagram, or listed in text.>

Subsystem Descriptions
<Include a brief description of each subsystem.>

Exhibit 7-2 Detailed Use Case Description Document Template

Use Case Name
<A brief description. Usually a paragraph or less.>

Actors
<A list of the actors who communicate with this use case.>

Priority
<How important is this use case to the project?>

Status
<At what point are we in developing this use case?>

Preconditions
<A list of conditions that must be true before the use case starts.>

Postconditions
<A list of conditions that must be true when the use case ends, no matter which scenario is executed.>

Extension Points
<If the use case has extension points, list them here.>

"Used" Use Cases
<If the use case uses other use cases, list them here.>

Flow of Events
<This could be a 97basic path and alternative paths, or the primary scenario.>

Exhibit 7-2   Detailed Use Case Description Document Template (*Continued*)

Activity Diagram

<An activity diagram of the flow of events, or some significant or complex part of the flow of events.>

User Interface

<For systems that interface with people, include a description of the user interface, possibly using storyboards.>

Secondary Scenarios

<If alternatives and exceptions are not shown in the flow of events, scenarios should be listed here, and a brief description may be included.>

Sequence Diagrams

<If you don't have separate documents for scenarios, you might include sequence diagrams for them here.>

Subordinate Use Cases

<If the use case has subordinate use cases, show them here. Or you could include a use case diagram for the subordinate use cases. Or both. Also tell what subsystem is responsible for this subordinate use case.>

View of Participating Classes

<A collaboration showing all the classes whose objects interact to implement this use case. You also can show interfaces to the use case here and which of the classes implement the interfaces.>

Other Artifacts

<This can include references to the subsystem the use case belongs to, an analysis model, a design model, code, or test plans.>

Other Requirements

<This section is where you can put nonfunctional requirements affecting the use case.>

You don't have to include all these sections. If your use cases are not this complex, then you don't need all these sections. You may find you want additional sections. That's fine. This is just a sample given as a starting point. If it works as is, use it; otherwise, modify as needed.

Tool Support for Use Case Documents

Unless you are writing use cases on paper with pen, pencil, crayon, or whatever, you will be looking for some kind of tool support for your use case documents. Consider your needs before buying tools. Use case documents could be done in desktop publishing tools such as FrameMaker, word processing tools such as Microsoft Word, spreadsheets such as Microsoft Excel, HTML pages or other Web-based formats, requirements management tools such as Requisite Pro, groupware such as Lotus Notes, or in e-mail programs. Or they may be stored in a relational database. Almost any tool can be used to generate and store use case documents, so you have to consider the needs of your team, project, and company.

Answer these questions before going tool shopping:

- Are you only looking for a way to record text?
- Do you need search capabilities?
- Do you need to share the documents with a small, a large, or geographically distributed team?
- What about report generation? What kinds of reports would you like to get about your use cases?
- Do you want to be able to hyperlink from one part of a document to another part or another document?
- Do the documents have to be able to be shared across multiple platforms?
- Do you need the ability to compose documents into books to get the right page numbering or chapter numbering across documents?
- What other tools might need to use what is in the use case documents? How do you integrate to those tools?

After answering these questions you will be prepared to evaluate the tools you already have, as well as tools you are considering buying. One last thing to consider is ease of use. Hard-to-use tools tend to sit on a shelf unless there are no other options. In this case you have many options, so look for something your team will use.

ORDER-PROCESSING SYSTEM USE CASES

In real life, the use cases for a small system will be fairly well worked out before work begins on building the system. Large systems tend to work more in parallel than in a linear fashion. This means some people will work on use cases, while others start building code for the use cases already completed. Because our order-processing system is relatively small, we have completed all the use cases for it before building the system. We have not detailed the scenarios, however. They seem pretty simple. If we find out later they are relatively complex, we can write out detailed descriptions.

The rest of this chapter is the use case documentation for the order-processing system. Don't feel you have to read all of it. Just browse a bit to get a feel for the documentation. Here are a few things to look for.

You'll see a lot of uses relationships between use cases, but no extends. *Uses* are found early in the process and allow you to show commonality between parts of the system. *Extends* tends to be added later, when you find some new requirement or functionality that extends the current system. Since we haven't built the first system yet, we don't have anything to extend.

We noticed that all of the use cases involving the customer actor required gaining access to the system. So we added a new use case called Login. But then we had to figure out its relationship to the other use cases. Our first thought was to have each of the other use cases start by using login. That feels comfortable if the system is a bunch of independent applications, each with its own interface. So we start the Place Order application, which calls Login as its first activity. We don't see this system that way, however. Instead, there is a common front end for logging into the application. Based on user selection, we branch to one of the other operations. As a result we have a branch in Login with uses relationships to the other use cases. You can see this results in a messy diagram. We might decide to rewrite the use case Login uses and put Login as a precondition of each one.

Look at the Login activity diagram (Exhibit 7-5) to see Branching shown as a decision point. The Place Order activity diagram (Exhibit 7-8) is an example of a way to show an alternative flow of events. This diagram also shows looping.

We're not entirely happy with the process for handling back-ordered items, but since it seems to work, we'll go with it for now. This is an area we'll plan to revisit later to make the process more efficient. Right now our focus is on getting a working system completed.

Look at what happened to some of the uses relationships. A use case must be completely contained within a system or subsystem, except for communicates relationships with actors. This means that we cannot have a uses relationship from a use case in one subsystem to a use case in another subsystem. The Place Order use case in the system diagram (Exhibit 7-3) uses the Give Product Information use case. But these use cases ended up in different subsystems—Place Order in the Manage Orders subsystem (Exhibit 7-26) and Give Product Information in the Product Info subsystem (Exhibit 7-23). Our uses relationship at the system level became a communicates relationship in the subsystems. You will see this in a number of places in the following pages.

ORDER-PROCESSING SYSTEM

We are developing order-processing software for a mail order company called National Widgets, which is a reseller of products purchased from various suppliers. Twice a year the company publishes a catalog of products, which is mailed to customers and other interested people.

Customers purchase products by submitting a list of products with payment to National Widgets. National Widgets fills the order and ships the products to the customer's address. The order-processing software will track the order from the time it is received until the product is shipped.

National Widgets will provide quick service. They should be able to ship a customer's order by the fastest, most efficient means possible. Customers may return items for restocking, but sometimes will pay a fee.

Risk Factors

- Will the inexperience of some of the software designers create problems?
- How can we prevent lost orders on system failure?
- How can we make the system easy for nontechnical people to use?
- Can we be successful if we don't support a Web interface?
- What if the system is immediately flooded with orders?
- How do we handle many simultaneous users in different parts of the company?
- How do we handle the database crashing?

SYSTEM-LEVEL USE CASES

Exhibit 7-3   Order-Processing Use Cases 1

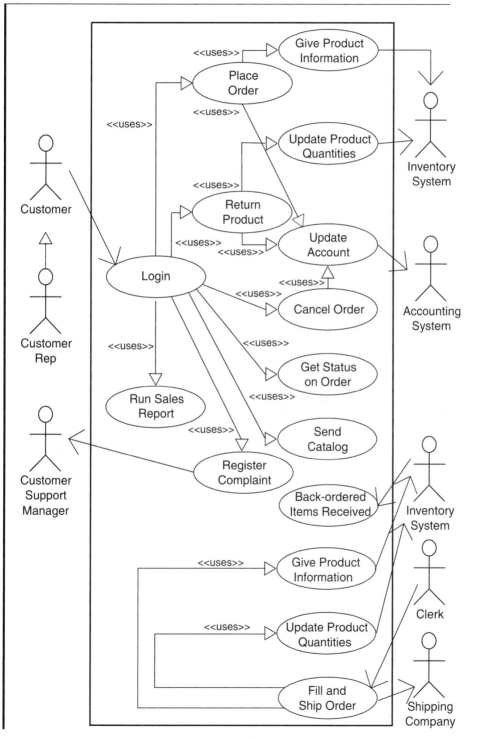

Architecture

Exhibit 7-4   Order-Processing Architecture

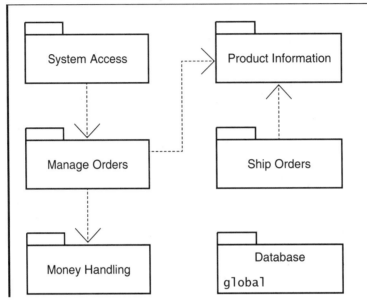

System Access Subsystem

This subsystem handles login and logout, and checks for access permissions.

Product Information Subsystem

This subsystem provides all kinds of information about products. It interfaces with the inventory system.

Manage Orders Subsystem

This subsystem handles order taking, product returns, order status, and order cancellation.

Ship Orders Subsystem

This subsystem prints pick lists for orders, generates mailing labels, and calculates shipping and handling for orders.

Money Handling Subsystem

This subsystem interfaces with the accounting system, updates accounts, charges and credits customers, and handles checks, credit cards, or money orders.

Database Subsystem

This subsystem contains the data we have to store for the application. It provides standard store, retrieve, update, and delete functions for the data that is stored.

LOGIN

This use case describes the process by which users log into the order-processing system. It also sets up access permissions for various categories of users.

Actors

- Customer

"Used" Use Cases

- Place Order
- Return Product
- Cancel Order
- Get Status on Order
- Send Catalog
- Register Complaint
- Run Sales Report

Flow of Events

Basic Path

1. The use case starts when the user starts the application.
2. The system will display the Login screen.
3. The user enters a username and password.
4. The system will verify the information.
5. The system will set access permissions.
6. The system will display the Main screen.
7. The user will select a function.
8. While the user does not select Exit loop
9. If the user selects Place Order then
    Use Place Order
10. else If the user selects Return Product then
    Use Return Product
11. else if the user selects Cancel Order then
    Use Cancel Order
12. else if the user selects Review Order then
    Use Get Status on Order
13. else if the user selects Send Catalog then
    Use Send Catalog
14. else if the user selects Contact Customer Service then
    Use Register Complaint
15. else if the user selects Run Sales Report and user is a Customer Rep then
    Use Run Sales Report

end if

16. The user will select a function.

end loop

17. The use case ends.

Activity Diagram

Exhibit 7-5 Login Primary Scenario

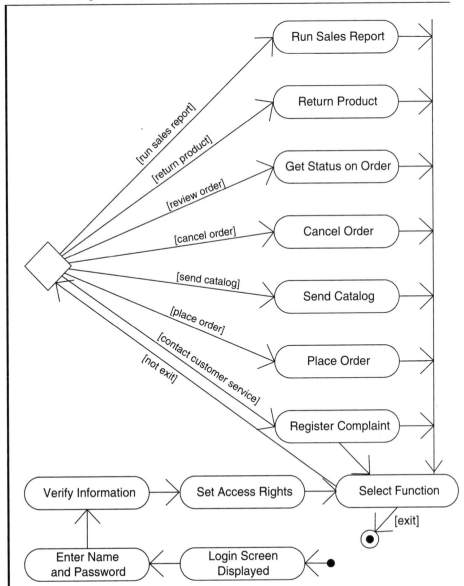

User Interface

Exhibit 7-6 Login Screen

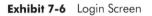

Welcome to National Widgets On-Line Catalog

Please Enter Your User Name and Password
to Access Our Electronic Catalog.

User Name

Password

Exhibit 7-7 Main Screen

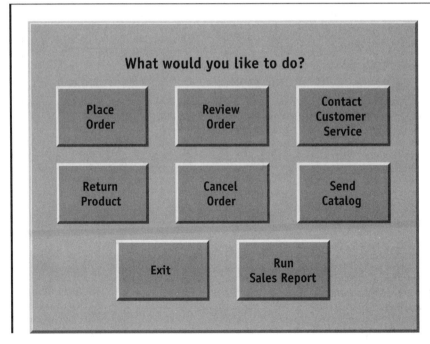

What would you like to do?

Place Order	Review Order	Contact Customer Service
Return Product	Cancel Order	Send Catalog
Exit	Run Sales Report	

Secondary Scenarios

- Bad user name
- Bad password
- User does not have a username and password for our system
- User selects a function for which she is not allowed access
- User makes no selection of function

Subordinate Use Cases

- System Access—Login
- Manage Orders—Display Main Screen

PLACE ORDER

This use case describes the process by which orders are entered into the order-processing system.

Actors

- Customer

"Used" Use Cases

- Give Product Information
- Update Account

Flow of Events

Basic Path

1. The use case starts when the customer selects Place Order.
2. The system displays the Place Order screen.
3. The customer enters his or her name and address.
4. The customer enters product codes for products to be ordered.
5. For each product code entered loop
   a) Use Give Product Information
   b) The system will add the price of the item to the total.
   end loop
6. The customer enters credit card payment information.
7. The customer selects Submit.
8. The system verifies the information and saves the order as pending.
9. Use Update Account
10. The order is marked confirmed, an order ID is returned to the customer, and the use case ends.

Alternative Paths. The customer can select Cancel at any time before selecting Submit. The order is not saved, and the use case ends.

Activity Diagram

Exhibit 7-8   Place Order Primary Scenario

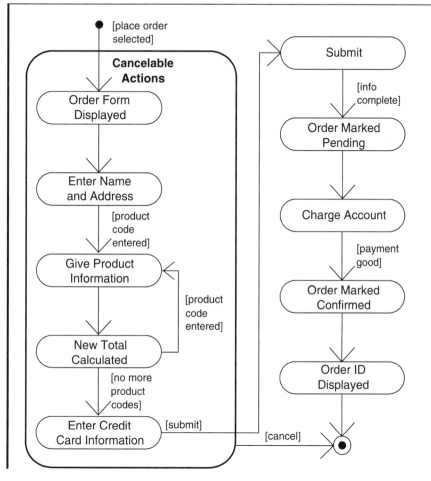

User Interface

Exhibit 7-9 Place Order Screen

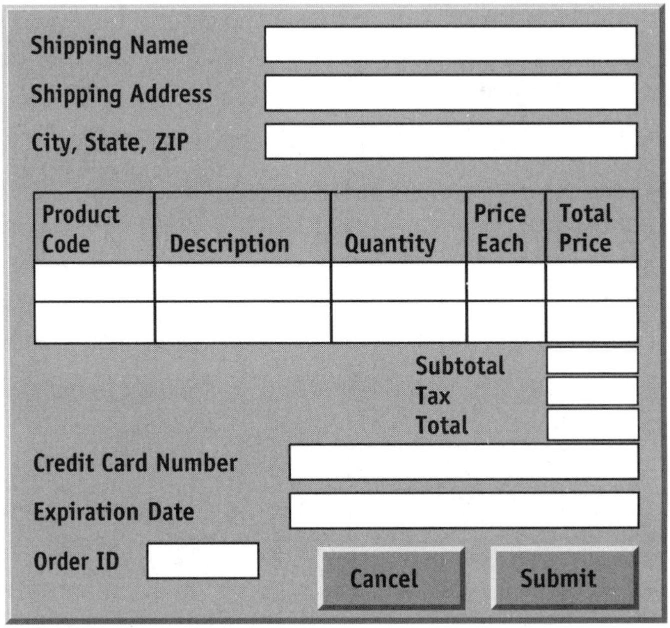

Secondary Scenarios

- Payment not there
- Shipping address incomplete
- Product code doesn't match actual products
- Product no longer carried
- Payment bad
- Customer pays by check
- Customer sends order by mail
- Customer phones in order

Subordinate Use Cases

- Manage Orders—Place Order
- Database—Save Order
- Database—Update Order

GIVE PRODUCT INFORMATION

This use case retrieves product information from the inventory system.

Actors

- Inventory system

"Used" Use Cases

- None

Flow of Events

Basic Path

1. This use case begins when a product code is entered.
2. The system sends a request to the inventory system for product information based on that product code.
3. The inventory system returns the product information, which must include at least a product description, price, and stock on hand.
4. The use case ends.

Activity Diagram

- None

User Interface

- None

Secondary Scenarios

- No such product
- Product no longer carried
- Inventory system unavailable

Subordinate Use Cases

- Product Info—Get Product Information

UPDATE ACCOUNT

This use case interacts with the accounting system to apply charges or credits to an account.

Actors

- Accounting system

"Used" Use Cases

- None

Flow of Events

Basic Path

1. The use case begins when a request to update an account is received.
2. The system will send credit card information and the amount of credit or debit to the accounting system.
3. The accounting system will send a status of Okay.
4. The use case ends.

Activity Diagram

- None

User Interface

- None

Secondary Scenarios

- Account overdrawn
- Account doesn't exist
- Accounting system not available

Subordinate Use Cases

- Money Handling—Update User Account

RETURN PRODUCT

This use case describes the process by which unwanted products are returned to the company by the customer.

Actors

- Customer rep

"Used" Use Cases

- Search For Order
- Update Product Quantities
- Update Account

Flow of Events

Basic Path

1. The use case starts when the customer rep selects Return Product.
2. Use Search for Order.
3. The system will display the selected order in the Return Products screen.
4. The customer rep will select the products to return.
5. The customer rep will select Submit.
6. Use Update Account.
7. Use Update Product Quantities.
8. The system will display an acknowledgment and the use case ends.

Activity Diagram

- None

User Interface

Exhibit 7-10 Return Products Screen

Shipping Name	AAA AAAA
Shipping Address	BBB BBBB
City, State, ZIP	CCC CCCC

Product Code	Description	Quantity to Return
XX	XXX	
XX	XXX	

Submit

Secondary Scenarios

- No orders for this customer
- Order ID not found in system
- Customer not found in system
- Account no longer valid
- Accounting system not available
- Inventory system not available

Subordinate Use Cases

- Manage Orders—Return Product
- Database—Update Order

SEARCH FOR ORDER

This use case describes the process for finding a particular order in the system.

Actors

- Customer

"Used" Use Cases

- None

Flow of Events

Basic Path

1. The use case starts when the Find Order screen is displayed.
2. The user enters an order ID or name and address.
3. The user selects Search.
4. If the user entered a name and address
    a) The system will display a list of orders for that customer, including at least an order ID and date of order
    b) The user will select one order.
    end if
5. The system returns an order ID and the use case ends.

Activity Diagram

- None

User Interface

Exhibit 7-11   Find Order Screen

Find Order

Shipping Name	
Shipping Address	
City, State, ZIP	

Or

Order ID	

Search

Exhibit 7-12   Order Selection Screen

Order ID	Date	Select
XX	XXX	
XX	XXX	

Select an Order

Secondary Scenarios

- No such customer
- No orders for customer
- No such order

Subordinate Use Cases

- Manage Orders—Search for Orders
- Database—Get Order List
- Database—Get Order

UPDATE PRODUCT QUANTITIES

This use case interfaces with the inventory system to update product quantities in the inventory.

Actors

- Inventory system

"Used" Use Cases

- None

Flow of Events

Basic Path

1. The use case starts when a request to update product quantities is received.
2. If the quantity is positive then
    The system will send a request to the inventory system to add that amount to the stock on hand for a product.
3. Otherwise
    The system will send a request to the inventory system to subtract that amount from the stock on hand for a product.
end if
4. The inventory system will send an acknowledgment, and the use case ends.

Activity Diagram

- None

User Interface

- None

Secondary Scenarios

- Inventory system not available
- Product no longer stocked

Subordinate Use Cases

- Product Info—Update Product Quantities

CANCEL ORDER

This use case describes the process by which a customer can cancel an order.

Actors

- Customer

"Used" Use Cases

- Search for Order
- Update Account

Flow of Events

Basic Path

1. The use case starts when the customer selects Cancel Order.
2. Use Search for Order.
3. The system will display the Cancel Order screen for that order.
4. The customer will select Cancel.
5. If the order has not been shipped
   Use Update Account
6. Otherwise
   Display Return Policies screen.
end if
7. The use case ends.

Activity Diagram

- None

User Interface

Exhibit 7-13 Return Policies Screen

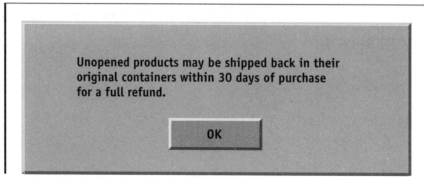

Unopened products may be shipped back in their original containers within 30 days of purchase for a full refund.

OK

Exhibit 7-14   Cancel Order Screen

Secondary Scenarios

- No orders for this customer
- Order ID not found in system
- Customer not found in system
- Account no longer valid
- Accounting system not available

Subordinate Use Cases

- Manage Orders—Cancel Order
- Database—Update Order

GET STATUS ON ORDER

This use case describes the process by which customers can get the current status on any of their orders.

Actors

- Customer

"Used" Use Cases

- Search for Order

Flow of Events

Basic Path

1. The use case starts when the user selects Review Order.
2. Use Search for Order.
3. The system will display the Get Status on Order screen, and the use case ends.

Activity Diagram

- None

User Interface

Exhibit 7-15   Get Status on Order Screen

Secondary Scenarios

- Order not found

Subordinate Use Cases

- Manage Orders—Get Status on Order

SEND CATALOG

This use case describes how a customer can request a catalog.

Actors

- Customer

"Used" Use Cases

- None

Flow of Events

Basic Path

1. The use case starts when the customer selects Send Catalog.
2. The Order Catalog screen is displayed.
3. The user enters a name and address.
4. The user selects Submit.
5. The request is submitted as a regular order with no charges to the system.
6. The use case ends.

Activity Diagram

- None

User Interface

Exhibit 7-16 Order Catalog Screen

Name	
Address	
City, State, ZIP	

Order Catalog [Submit]

Secondary Scenarios

- None

Subordinate Use Cases

- Manage Orders—Send Catalog
- Database—Save Order

REGISTER COMPLAINT

This use case describes how a customer can give feedback to the company.

Actors

- Customer
- Customer support manager

"Used" Use Cases

- None

Flow of Events

Basic Path

1. The use case starts when the user selects Contact Customer Service.
2. The Message screen is displayed.
3. The user enters text.
4. The user selects Submit.
5. The system sends the text entered in an e-mail message to the customer support manager, and the use case ends.

Activity Diagram

- None

User Interface

Exhibit 7-17   Message Screen

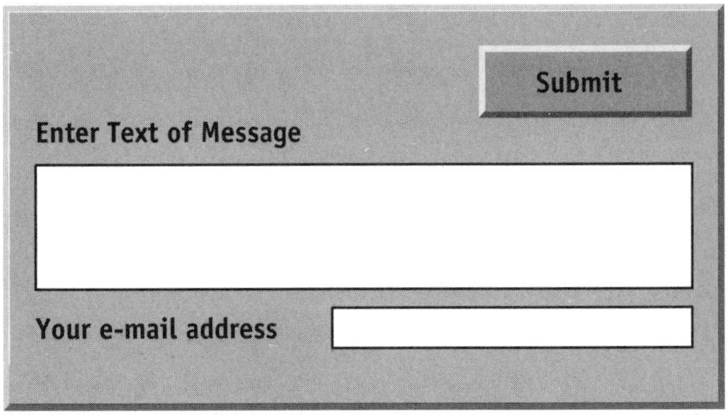

Secondary Scenarios

- None

Subordinated Use Cases

- Manage Orders—Register Complaint

RUN SALES REPORT

This use case describes how a customer rep can get reports on sales.

Actors

- Customer rep

"Used" Use Cases

- None

Flow of Events

Basic Path

1. The use case starts when the user selects Run Sales Report.
2. The Choose Report screen is displayed.
3. The user selects a report.
4. The user selects Submit.
5. The system displays the report, and the use case ends.

Activity Diagram

- None

User Interface

Exhibit 7-18   Report Selection Screen

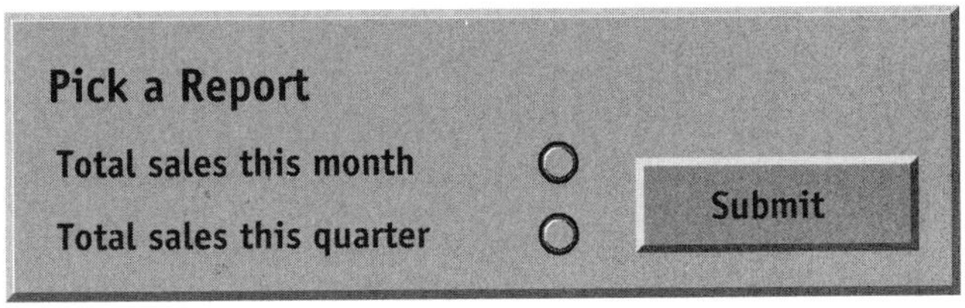

Secondary Scenarios

- None

Subordinate Use Cases

- Manage Orders—Run Sales Report
- Database—Get Sales Data

FILL AND SHIP ORDER

This use case describes how a warehouse clerk gets information on what orders to fill, their products, and the addresses for shipping.

Actors

- Clerk

"Used" Use Cases

- Give Product Info
- Update Product Quantities

Flow of Events

Basic Path

1. The use case starts when the clerk starts the fill-and-ship-order application.
2. The system displays the Fill Order screen with a list of all confirmed orders.
3. While the clerk selects an order
   a) The system displays the order
   b) For all the items in the order loop
      1) Use Give Product Information
      2) The system displays stock on hand information for the item
      3) If the item is out of stock
         a. The system marks the item back-ordered.
         b. The system sends a backorder request to the inventory system.
         c. The order is marked back-orders.
         end if
      end loop
   c) If there are items that are not back-ordered and not shipped then
      1) For each such item loop
         a. Use Update Product Quantities
         b. Print item and quantity on packing slip
         c. mark item shipped.
         end loop
      2) If all items are marked shipped
            mark the order shipped.
         end if
      3) The system calculates postage due

4) The system prints a mailing label with the shipping address and postage due

5) The system sends a notice to the shipping company that packages are ready to be picked up.

end if

end loop

4. The use case ends

Activity Diagram

• None

User Interface

Exhibit 7-19 Orders to Fill Screen

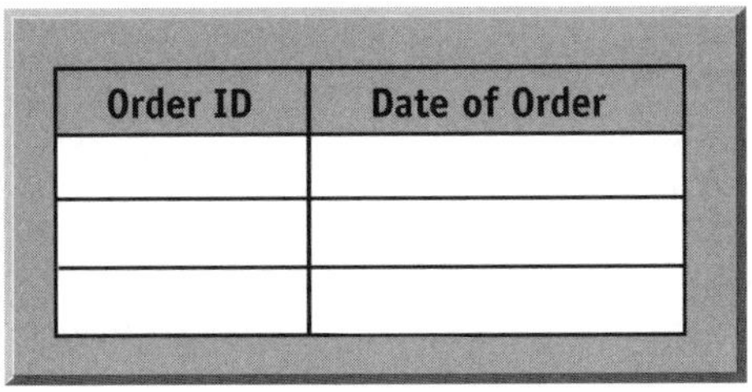

Order ID	Date of Order

Exhibit 7-20 Order with Stock on Hand Screen

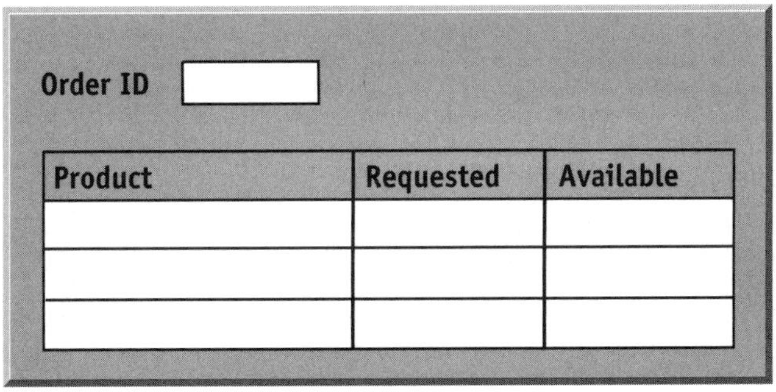

Order ID [   ]

Product	Requested	Available

Secondary Scenarios

- Inventory system not available
- Printer not available
- Shipping company not available

Subordinate Use Cases

- Ship Orders—Ship and Fill Order
- Database—Get Order List
- Database—Get Order
- Database—Update Order
- Product Info—Back-order Item

BACK-ORDERED ITEMS RECEIVED

This use case describes what happens when a shipment of items is received for which the company has back-orders.

Actors

- Inventory system

"Used" Use Cases

- None

Flow of Events

Basic Path

1. The use case starts when the inventory system notifies the system that back-ordered items have been received.
2. The system finds all orders marked back-orders and changes their status to confirmed.
3. For each item marked back-ordered, clear its state.
4. The use case ends.

Activity Diagram

- None

User Interface

- None

Secondary Scenarios

- None

Subordinate Use Cases

- Product Info—Back-ordered Items Received
- Database—Get Order List
- Database—Update Order

SYSTEM ACCESS SUBSYSTEM

This subsystem handles login and logout, and checks for access permissions.

System Access Use Cases

Exhibit 7-21 System Access Use Cases

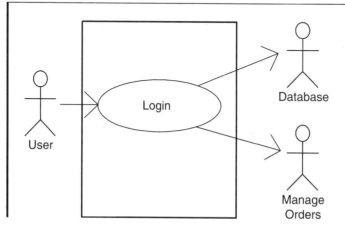

System Access Architecture

Exhibit 7-22 System Access Boundary

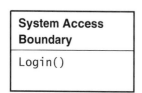

Login Subordinate Use Case

Basic Path

1. The use case starts when the user starts the application.
2. The system displays the Login screen.
3. The user enters a user name and password.
4. The system asks the database for a user record for the user name.
5. The system validates the login based on information from the user record.
6. The system sets access levels for the user.
7. The system asks Manage Orders to display the main screen.
8. The use case ends.

PRODUCT INFORMATION SUBSYSTEM

This subsystem provides all kinds of information about products. It interfaces with the inventory system.

Product Information Use Cases

Exhibit 7-23 Product Information Use Cases

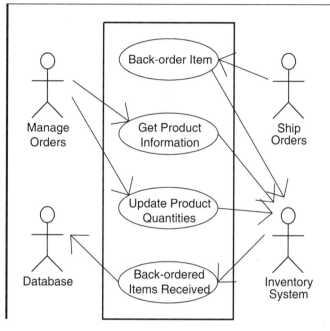

Product Information Architecture

Exhibit 7-24 Product Information Boundary

Product Information Facade
GetProductInfo(Product code)
UpdateProductQuantities(Product, Quantity)
MarkProductBack-ordered(Product, Quantity)
Back-orderedItemsArrived ()

Get Product Info Subordinate Use Case

Basic Path

1. This use case begins when an actor requests product information.
2. The system sends a request to the inventory system for product information based on that product code.
3. The Inventory System returns the product information, which must include at least a product description, price, and stock on hand.
4. The use case ends.

Update Product Quantities Subordinate Use Case

Basic Path

1. The use case starts when a request to Update Product Quantities is received.
2. If the quantity is positive then
    the system will send a request to the inventory system to add that amount to the stock on hand for a product.
3. Otherwise
    the system will send a request to the inventory system to subtract that amount from the stock on hand for a product.
end if
4. The Inventory System sends an acknowledgment, and the use case ends.

Back-order Item Subordinate Use Case

Basic Path

1. The use case starts when a request to back-order items is received.
2. The system sends a request to the Inventory System to place an order for out-of-stock items.
3. The Inventory System sends an acknowledgment, and the use case ends.

Back-Ordered Items Received Subordinate Use Case

Basic Path

1. The use case starts when the Inventory System notifies the system that back-ordered items have been received.
2. The system requests the database to find all orders marked back-orders.
3. For each order returned
    a) The system changes its status to confirmed.
    b) For each item marked back-ordered
        The system will clear its state.
end loop
    c) The system requests the database to update the order.
end loop
4. The use case ends.

MANAGE ORDERS SUBSYSTEM

This subsystem handles order taking, product return, order status, and order cancelations.

Manage Orders Architecture

Exhibit 7-25 Manage Orders Boundary

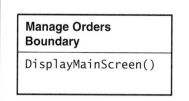

Manage Orders Use Cases

Exhibit 7-26 Manage Orders Use Cases

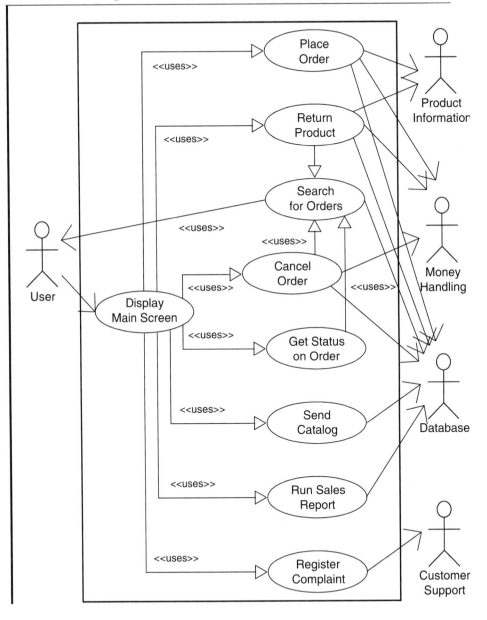

Display Main Screen Subordinate Use Case

Basic Path

1. The use case begins when System Access requests the main screen be displayed.
2. The system will display the main screen.
3. The user will select a function.
4. While the user does not select Exit loop
5. If the user selects Place Order then
     use Place Order.
6. else if the user selects Return Product then
     use Return Product.
7. else if the user selects Cancel Order then
     use Cancel Order.
8. else if the user selects Review Order then
     use Get Status on Order.
9. else if the user selects Send Catalog then
     use Send Catalog.
10. else if the user selects Contact Customer Service then
     use Register Complaint.
11. else if the user selects Run Sales Report and user is a customer rep then
     use Run Sales Report.
end if
12. The user will select a function.
end loop
13. The use case ends.

Place Order Subordinate Use Case

Basic Path

1. The use case starts when a Place Order request is received.
2. The system displays the Place Order screen.
3. The customer enters his or her name and address.
4. The customer enters product codes for products to be ordered.
5. For each product code entered
   a) The system requests product information from Product Information.
   b) The system adds the price of the item to the total.
end
6. The customer enters credit card payment information.
7. The customer selects Submit.
8. The system verifies the information.
9. The system marks the order pending.
10. The system asks the database to save the order.
11. The system asks Money Handling to update the user account.
12. The system marks the order confirmed.
13. The system asks the database to update the order.
14. The system displays an order ID to the customer, and the use case ends.

Alternative Paths. At any time before selecting Submit, the customer can select Cancel. The order is not saved, and the use case ends.

Return Product Subordinate Use Case

Basic Path

1. The use case starts when a Return Product request is received.
2. Use Search for Order.
3. The system will display the selected order on the Return Products screen.
4. The customer rep will select the products to return.
5. The customer rep will select Submit.
6. The system will request Money Handling to update the user account.
7. The system will request Product Information to Update Product Quantities.
8. The system will request the database to update the order.
9. The system will display an acknowledgment, and the use case ends.

Search for Orders Subordinate Use Case

Basic Path

1. The use case starts when a Find Order request is received.
2. The system displays the Find Order screen.
3. The user enters an order ID or name and address.
4. The user selects Search.
5. If the user entered a name and address
    a) The system will ask the database for a list of order for the customer.
    b) The system will display a list of orders for that customer, including at least an order ID and date of order.
    c) The user will select one order.
end if
6. The system asks the database for an order record.
7. The system returns an order ID, and the use case ends.

Cancel Orders Subordinate Use Case

Basic Path

1. The use case starts when a Cancel Order request is received.
2. Use Search for Order.
3. The system will display the Cancel Order screen for that order.
4. The customer will select Cancel.
5. If the order has not been shipped
    a) The system will request Money Handling to update the user account.
    b) The system will mark the order canceled.
    c) The system will request the database to update the order.
6. Otherwise
    display Return Policies Screen.
end if
7. The use case ends.

Get Status on Order Subordinate Use Case

Basic Path

1. The use case starts when a Get Status request is received.
2. Use Search for Order.
3. The system will display the Order Status screen, and the use case ends.

Send Catalog Subordinate Use Case

Basic Path

1. The use case starts when a Send Catalog request is received.
2. The Catalog Order screen is displayed.
3. The user enters a name and address.
4. The user selects Submit.
5. The system creates an order with a product of Catalog and no charges.
6. The system requests the database to save the order.
7. The use case ends.

Register Complaint Subordinate Use Case

Basic Path

1. The use case starts when a request to contact customer service is received.
2. The Message screen is displayed.
3. The user enters text.
4. The user selects Submit.
5. The system sends the text entered in an e-mail message to the customer-support manager, and the use case ends.

Run Sales Report Subordinate Use Case

Basic Path

1. The use case starts when a Run Sales Report request is received.
2. The Choose Report screen is displayed.
3. The user selects a report.
4. The Message screen is displayed.
5. The user selects Submit.
6. The system requests sales data from the database.
7. The system displays the report, and the use case ends.

SHIP ORDERS SUBSYSTEM

This subsystem prints pick lists for orders, generates mailing labels, and calculates shipping and handling for orders.

Ship Orders Use Cases

Exhibit 7-27   Ship Orders Use Cases

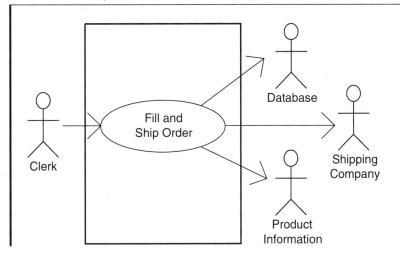

Ship Orders Architecture

Exhibit 7-28   Ship Orders Boundary

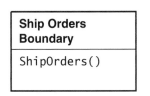

Fill and Ship Order Subordinate Use Case

Basic Path

1. The use case starts when the clerk starts the Fill and Ship Order application.
2. The system displays the Fill Order screen.
3. The system requests the database for a list of confirmed orders, by order ID.
4. While the clerk selects an order
   a) The system requests the database for the order.
   b) The system displays the order
   c) For all the items in the order loop
      1) The system requests stock-on-hand information from Product Information.
      2) The system displays stock-on-hand information for the item
      3) If the item is out of stock
         a. the system marks the item back-ordered.
         b. the system requests Product Information to back-order the items.
         c. the order is marked back-ordered.
         end if
      end loop
   d) If there are items that are not back-ordered and not shipped then
      1) For each such item loop
         a. the system requests Product Information to Update Product Quantities.
         b. the system will print item and quantity on packing slip.
         c. the system will mark the item shipped.
      end loop
      2) If all items are marked shipped
            the system will mark the order shipped.
   end if
      3) The system calculates postage due.
      4) The system prints a mailing label with the shipping address and postage due.
      5) The system sends a notice to the shipping company that packages are ready to be picked up.
   end if
   e) The system requests the database to update the order.
end loop
5. The use case ends.

MONEY HANDLING SUBSYSTEM

This subsystem interfaces to the accounting system; updates accounts; charges and credits customers; and handles checks, credit cards, or money orders.

Money Handling Use Cases

Exhibit 7-29 Money Handling Use Cases

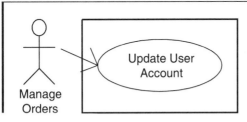

Money Handling Architecture

Exhibit 7-30 Money Handling Boundary

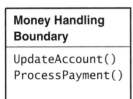

Update User Account Subordinate Use Case

Basic Path

1. The use case begins when Manage Orders requests that an account be updated.
2. The system will send credit card information and the amount of credit or debit to Accounting System.
3. The Accounting System will send a status of Okay.
4. The use case ends.

DATABASE SUBSYSTEM

This subsystem contains the data that we need to store for the application. It provides standard store, retrieve, update, and delete functions for the data that is stored.

Database Use Cases

Exhibit 7-31   Database Use Cases

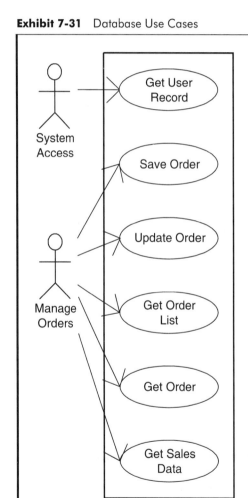

All these use cases are very similar. We show one as an example.

Get User Record Subordinate Use Case

Basic Path

1. The use case starts when System Access requests a user record.
2. The system locates the user record using the username.
3. The system returns the user record to System Access.
4. The use case ends.

Database Architecture

Exhibit 7-32   Database Boundary

Database Boundary

```
GetUserRecord(Username)
SaveOrder(Order)
UpdateOrder(Order)
GetOrderList(CustomerInfo)
GetOrder(OrderId)
GetSalesData(month)
GetSalesData(territory)
GetOrderList(confirmed)
```

CHAPTER REVIEW

We have not developed any new material for our order-processing system in this chapter. But we have organized our material to make it easier to read, review, and maintain. You are not required to have documented your complete system at this point. You need enough information to develop a project plan and start on the first iteration of construction.

Table 7-1 Elaboration Phase Deliverables

Complete	Deliverables
✔	Detailed primary scenarios
✔	Secondary scenarios
✔	Activity diagrams
✔	User interface diagrammed (optional)
✔	Architecture
	Project plan

Chapter 8

Use Cases and the Project Plan

Before we actually can build the system, we need a plan of attack. What will be worked on first? How do we know something is complete? We will rely on use cases to develop the project plan for our system.

The final thing to develop in elaboration is the first project plan. Like our other documents, this will be updated over time to reflect knowledge gained as we work on the project. The primary documents you will use for this are the risk factors, market factors, list of assumptions, and all the use cases.

PLANNING THE PROJECT

The project plan will be based on iterations. An iteration is some piece of the project that can be analyzed, designed, coded, integrated, and tested. Each iteration produces working code. Each iteration adds pieces to the system until the system is complete.

Using this approach we integrate often, test often, and always have some amount of code that works. If a project gets to a point where it is obvious that some requirements will not be completed, there is always a working version that can be polished and delivered—the last complete iteration.

Start by determining how many iterations you will have in construction. A couple of factors have to be taken into account. You have to consider the length of the project. In general you will have more iterations in longer projects. Also consider your company's environment. What is a comfortable amount of time for your team to go through a complete development cycle? Each iteration should be about the same duration, perhaps two weeks, perhaps two months, perhaps six months. You might determine the length of an iteration by planning the first one, then estimating the time to build it. That will be the basic length of your iterations. The iteration length sets up a heart-beat for your project, a rhythm that your team will depend on. As you figure out what goes into each iteration, you may need to adjust the duration a bit. But all the iterations should be close to the same length.

Now you know how many iterations you will have and how long each one is. Next you need to plan the contents of the iterations. The prioritized list of risks is the key document for planning the contents of the iterations. Make sure this list is up to date and the priorities are feasible. Be sure to consider assumptions made and market factors when assigning priorities. These could be very important to the success of your project.

Now that you have a complete, prioritized list of risks for your project, look at the top risks. These are things that will cause project failure if they are not addressed. Now look at the use cases and determine which ones handle the risks you have identified. Those are the use cases you will implement in the first iteration in the construction phase. Repeat this process with the next-highest risks for the second iteration. Continue scheduling until you have filled up all your iterations with use cases to develop.

Very likely you will develop only some of the scenarios for a use case in any particular iteration. Other scenarios will be completed in other iterations. Unless the system is quite small, you will use the subordinate use cases for planning purposes. You want to find a piece of the system that will imple-ment some complete piece of functionality, although not necessarily all of its alternatives and exceptions.

Some additional things besides risk must be considered when planning the project. Your first couple of iterations should implement the core func-tionality of your system. You want to include things like using a database, CORBA, or a network fairly early on. You might decide to build a simulator in the first iteration to represent things you won't have until later. For example, you may be building some software to control hardware. The hardware isn't actually built yet, so you create a simulator that has the same interface as the hardware so that the software can be built and tested.

Frequently, the first iteration has fewer features and fewer scenarios implemented because you have to develop a lot of the supporting software. On the other hand, most of the work in the last iteration is to add new fea-tures. Adjust the work in each iteration to match the duration you decided on for the iteration.

In this first planning stage, it is better to have more work planned in the first couple of iterations and let the last iteration be light on functionality. You will find more work as you go along, which will be added to the last iteration.

You also may find you have overestimated what you can accomplish, so you will end up moving work from an early iteration to a later one.

You will find it relatively easy to plan the first two iterations. The others will be more vague. That is okay. As you work through each iteration, you will get a better understanding of your system and your team, and will be able to update the plans for later iterations accordingly.

In addition to all the other planning, you also will need to define the goal of the iteration. What are you trying to accomplish? How will you know if you have succeeded? Add this kind of information to your planning document.

Let's look at an example for our order-processing system.

"Hey, Gus, how much longer before we can start writing software?"

"Just as soon as we plan our approach to putting this system together."

"More documentation," Dennis muttered. "We're never going to get done unless we start!"

"Well then, where would you start?" asked Gus, smiling at the others.

"Oh, I don't know. I've been thinking of the flow so long I forgot about the programming. Why don't we just pick a place and start writing code? I want to think I'm doing something!"

"Well then, how about this? Why don't we list the use cases in the order we think they are important, then look at what we need to make the first one work?"

"Oh! I got it!" Lisa called out. "If we do that, then the most important parts are likely to be finished first, because we have to have them working to finish the use case! That's great!"

"But how do we know which is the most important?" Tara added. "Do we just pick the longest one and start there?"

"Actually, no. The longest one might not include the biggest risks."

"Oh! That's what you're going to do with that list! I wondered about that."

"Yes, that list is one of the things we'll use to decide which use case is most important. And for our first iteration, we want to cover the most important things."

"First iteration?" Dennis said. "Why don't we just make a plan for the whole thing and start writing it?"

"Well, I can think of a very good reason right here. Why are we having this conversation?"

"Because I'm tired of just writing documents and want to get working! I want to see something actually get done!"

"Right! Getting something done is a great feeling. So, by breaking our system down into smaller steps, which we call iterations, we'll be able to write code and test it. We'll be able to see things get done."

"Oh. Instead of waiting until the whole project is done before we can see something tested and working, we can see pieces of it working now."

"Right! And each iteration gives us more confidence in our project because we'll use the riskiest use cases first. If they don't work, we still can change our use cases and architecture before we've wasted too much time. Here is our current list of use cases. What should we do first?

- Login
- Place Order
- Return Product
- Give Product Information
- Update Account
- Update Product Quantities
- Cancel Order
- Find Order
- Get Status on Order
- Send Catalog
- Register Complaint
- Run Sales Report
- Backordered Items received
- Give Product Information
- Update Product Quantities
- Fill and Ship Order

"Well, login isn't important if we don't allow customers direct access. But I think we should do Place Order early so we have something in the database for the other use cases to use."

"That means we have to include Give Product Information and Update Account. And we will have coded the interfaces to both those other pieces of software. Sounds like plenty for a first iteration."

"I want to add Get Status on Order."

"Why?"

" ' Cause Place Order just puts something into the database. I want to be able to get something back out to check it."

"Good idea."

Iteration 1—Deadline Sept. 22

Goals for the Iteration:

We will have the basics of ordering a product worked out, including the interfaces to the accounting and inventory systems. This will set up the framework of communication between all parts of our system, from the user interface, to the other software systems, and to the database.

- Order Product, primary scenario only
- Give Product Information, primary scenario only
- Update Account, primary scenario only
- Get Status on Order, primary scenario only

"Hey, why only primary scenarios?"

"Because we have enough to do as it is. There is a bunch of stuff to work out so multiple people can use the system at the same time. What looks easy on the surface has a whole framework of software behind it that everything in our system will use. We'll do the scenarios in a later iteration, after we have the basic system working. What next?"

"Let's do Fill and Ship. It's the rest of the order cycle and lets us check that the product quantities are getting updated properly."

"Want to do the backordered stuff too?"

"Sure."

Iteration 2—Deadline Oct. 13

Goals for the Iteration:

In this iteration we will implement the order-filling half of the process. This will complete the interfaces to the inventory system and will introduce an interface to the shipping companies.

- Fill and Ship Order, primary scenario
- Update Product Quantities, primary scenario
- Back-ordered Items Received, primary scenario

"Most of the rest is really easy, now that we have the basic framework. The only one at all complicated is Return Product."

"Okay. Let's put it all into Iteration 3, then add a final iteration for the scenarios."

Iteration 3—Deadline Nov. 3

Goals for the Iteration:

At the end of this iteration, we will have completed all the primary scenarios. We will be ready to start taking and filling orders.

- Login, primary scenario
- Return Product, primary scenario
- Cancel Order, primary scenario
- Find Order, primary scenario
- Send Catalog, primary scenario
- Register Complaint, primary scenario
- Run Sales Report, primary scenario

Iteration 4—Deadline Nov. 24

Goals for the Iteration:

At the end of this iteration, we will have completed the order-processing system.

- All secondary scenarios
- All error handling functionality

You can see that the later iterations include more functionality than the first. This allows the team to develop the basic mechanisms of the system first, with just a few functions to test it. Later iterations will depend on those mechanisms working. Some things you may need to develop early include error handling, interprocess communication, communication across networks, interfacing with a database, or transaction processing.

A benefit to this risk-driven, iterative approach becomes apparent on projects that cannot meet their final deadline. They still are able to deliver a working system with the most important functionality in place, tested, and working. Features that could not be included by the deadline could be planned for a next release of the product.

Build versus Buy Decisions

In planning the project you need to consider if the team will build the whole system or if some components will be bought or reused from previous projects. Perhaps some of the software is being developed by another company or another division of your company.

Buying a piece of your system will save in development time and may cost less than building it. On the other hand, costs will be associated with integrating that software into your project. Some kinds of things you can buy include libraries of functions, databases and repositories, libraries of domain-specific elements, and special-purpose tools such as parsers, search engines, forms, spreadsheets, bug tracking systems, and so on. You also may be able to outsource work such as customer support, payroll, or order gathering.

"Hey, Lisa," Tara said. "How much time do you think it will take to write a database?"

"What? Hold it!" called Gus, leaning across the table. "Who said we are going to write a database?"

"Well, don't we have to? It's referenced here in the Place Order use case."

"We don't want to write a database! There are lots of them on the market, let's just buy one."

"But wouldn't that mean we are dependent on someone outside our company?"

"Yes, but I think that will be a smaller risk that writing one ourselves. If we pick the right database, we can get support from the manufacturer. Remember, our business is to take and fill orders. I'd rather spend time doing that than working on something we can buy! Besides, it'll be much faster."

"That's true," Dennis added. "If we purchase one, we just have to write the interface to it. That's got to be a lot faster than writing an entire database by ourselves, and we'd have to interface to it anyway. Let's buy one. It seems the best route."

"But what happens if they go out of business? Do we have to start over?"

"Nope! Remember the operations we put in front of the database subsystem? Because we did that, the only thing that knows we have changed databases is the database subsystem. None of our other software has to change! That's why we defined those subsystem operations early."

Risks are associated with buying; for example:

- How reputable is the company you are buying from?
- How good are their systems?
- How long have they been in business?
- Who are their customers?
- If this company goes out of business, how hard would it be to replace this software with something new?
- Are there industry standards for the system you want to buy?
- Does a particular system adhere to these standards?
- How are you going to interface to this system? Do you need to add processes or software to implement the interface?
- How long will it take to learn to use it?

Compare these risks to the risks of building the system yourself by asking yourself the following questions:

- How good are my people?
- Do they have or can they learn the skills needed?
- Do we have enough time in the schedule to build this piece?
- Do we have enough money to build it?

If you decide to buy, include these risks in your project risks and include the integration of purchased components into the project schedule.

Prototyping

You may want to build some prototypes during elaboration to try out some ideas or determine if a high risk feature is possible. These prototypes are not production-level code and even may be written in a language different from the one your project will use. Though you may decide to include pieces of the prototype in your project, they are essentially throw-away code.

As a result of the prototyping effort, you may decide that a certain feature is not feasible and remove it from the project. If that feature is key to the project, you even may decide to abandon the project. Better to make that decision now, than after a couple of years of development.

You might decide that what you are trying to accomplish in the prototype is feasible, but you will have to do it a different way. That may mean making changes to some or all of the documentation you have produced, including the project schedule.

ESTIMATING WORK WITH USE CASES

In 1993 Gustav Karner of Objectory AB, later acquired by Rational Software Corporation, did some research into estimating man-hours for project completion based on use cases. His work is a modification of the work by Albrecht on function points. Karner's results are promising. We are including his estimating method here if you want to use it as a starting point for determining the amount of work for your project. Our thanks to Rational Software Corporation for allowing us to include the research in this book.

This method is preliminary and should be used with other estimating methods, such as function points or COCOMO, to get an idea of the number of man-months for your project. We are interested in hearing how well it works for you or what you would change to make it fit your projects better. We have included a response form in Appendix D.

Weighting Actors

You will start the process by considering the actors for your system. For each actor, determine whether it is simple, average, or complex. A simple actor represents another system with a defined application programming interface. An average actor is either another system that interacts through a protocol such as TCP/IP, or it is a person interacting through a text-based interface (such as an old ASCII terminal). A complex actor is a person interacting through a graphical user interface (see Table 8-1).

Count how many of each kind of actor you have. Then multiply each type by a weighting factor. The number of simple actors will be multiplied by 1, the number of average actors by 2, and the number of complex actors by 3. Add these products together to get a total.

For our order-processing system, we find the following:

- Customer—complex
- Inventory system—simple
- Accounting system—simple
- Customer service manager—average
- Customer rep—complex
- Clerk—complex
- Shipping company—average

Table 8-1   Actor Weighting Factors

Actor type	Description	Factor
Simple	Program interface	1
Average	Interactive, or protocol-driven interface	2
Complex	Graphical interface	3

Table 8-1 indicates the following:

> 2 simple * 1 = 2
>
> 2 average * 2 = 4
>
> 3 complex * 3 = 9
>
> Total actor weight for order processing 2 + 4 + 9 = 15

Weighting Use Cases

Now we do a similar process for the list of use cases. You don't need to consider used use cases or extending use cases. For each use case determine whether it is simple, average, or complex. The basis of this decision is the number of transactions in a use case, including secondary scenarios. For this purpose, a transaction is defined to be an atomic set of activities, which is either performed entirely or not at all. A simple use case has 3 or fewer transactions, an average use case has 4 to 7 transactions, and a complex use case has more than 7 transactions (see Table 8-2).

We haven't talked about classes yet, which are another mechanism for measuring use case complexity. If you already have picked out analysis classes for your system and determined which ones are used to implement a particular use case, you can use the information in place of transactions to determine use case complexity. We consider only analysis classes at this time, not classes that we will add during design.

Table 8-2   Transaction-Based Weighting Factors

Use case type	Description	Factor
Simple	3 or fewer transactions	5
Average	4 to 7 transactions	10
Complex	More than 7 transactions	15

Table 8-3 Analysis Class-Based Weighting Factors

Use case type	Description	Factor
Simple	Fewer than 5 analysis classes	5
Average	5 to 10 analysis classes	10
Complex	More than 10 analysis classes	15

A simple use case can be implemented with fewer than 5 analysis classes, an average use case can be implemented with 5 to 10 analysis classes, and a complex use case can be implemented with more than 10 analysis classes (see Table 8-3). We will look at classes and how they relate to use cases in Chapter 10.

Count how many of each kind of use case you have. Then multiply each type by a weighting factor. The number of simple use cases will be multiplied by 5, the number of average use cases by 10, and the number of complex use cases by 15. Add these products together to get a total.

For our order-processing system, we find the following:

- Place order—average
- Return product—average
- Cancel order—simple
- Get status on order—simple
- Send catalog—simple
- Run sales report—simple
- Register complaint—simple
- Fill and ship order—average
- Back-ordered items received—average

Using either Table 8-2 or Table 8-3, we find the following:

    5 simple * 5 = 25

    4 average * 10 = 40

    0 complex * 15 = 0

    Total use case weight for order processing 25 + 40 + 0 = 65

Add the total for actors to the total for use cases to get the unadjusted use case points (UUCP). This raw number will be adjusted to reflect your project's complexity and the experience of the people on the project.

For order processing, we have:

    15 + 65 = 80 UUCP

Weighting Technical Factors

We have an idea of the complexity of the use cases and interfaces. Now we need to weight the UUCP for factors such as the complexity of the project and the experience levels of the people on the project.

Start by calculating the technical complexity of the project. This is called the technical complexity factor (TCF). To calculate the TCF, go through Table 8-4 and rate each factor from 0 to 5. A rating of 0 means the factor is irrelevant for this project, 5 means it is essential. Now, for each factor multiply its rating by its weight from the table. Finally, add together all these numbers to get the total T factors.

$$\text{TFactor} = \sum (\text{Tlevel}) \bullet (\text{WeightingFactor})$$
$$\text{TCF} \quad = 0.6 + (0.01 \bullet \text{TFactor})$$

Let's rate the factors for National Widgets (Table 8-5). Now add all the extended values together

$$0 + 3 + 5 + 1 + 0 + 2.5 + 2.5 + 0 + 3 + 5 + 3 + 5 + 0 = 30$$

Plugging that into our formula, we get:

$$\text{TCF} = 0.6 + (0.01 * 30) = 0.9$$

Table 8-4   Technical Factors for System and Weights

Factor number	Factor description	Weight
T1	Distributed system	2
T2	Response or throughput performance objectives	1
T3	End-user efficiency (online)	1
T4	Complex internal processing	1
T5	Code must be reusable	1
T6	Easy to install	0.5
T7	Easy to use	0.5
T8	Portable	2
T9	Easy to change	1
T10	Concurrent	1
T11	Includes special security features	1
T12	Provides direct access for third parties	1
T13	Special user training facilities are required	1

Table 8-5 National Widgets Numbers

Factor number	Weight	Assigned value	Extended value	Reason
T1	2	0	0	Not planning on distributing first release
T2	1	3	3	Speed is likely limited by human input
T3	1	5	5	Needs to be efficient
T4	1	1	1	Easy processing
T5	1	0	0	Nice, but later
T6	0.5	5	2.5	Needs to be easy for non-technical people
T7	0.5	5	2.5	Needs to be easy for non-technical people
T8	2	0	0	Not at this time
T9	1	3	3	Sure
T10	1	5	5	Not exactly, but it is multiuser
T11	1	3	3	Simple security
T12	1	5	5	Customers
T13	1	0	0	So easy, we don't need training

Now consider the experience level of the people on the project. This is called the environmental factor (EF). To calculate EF, go through Table 8-6 and rate each factor from 0 to 5. For factors F1 through F4, 0 means no experience in the subject, 5 means expert, 3 means average. For F5, 0 means no motivation for the project, 5 means high motivation, 3 means average. For F6, 0 means extremely unstable requirements, 5 means unchanging requirements, 3 means average. For F7, 0 means no part-time technical staff, 5 means all part-time technical staff, 3 means average. For F8, 0 means easy-to-use programming language, 5 means very difficult programming language, 3 means average.

Now, for each factor, multiply its rating by its weight from the table. Finally, add all the numbers together to get the total F factors.

$$\text{EFactor} = \sum (\text{Flevel}) \bullet (\text{WeightingFactor})$$
$$\text{EF} = 1.4 + (-0.03 \bullet \text{EFactor})$$

Table 8-6 Environmental Factors for Team and Weights

Factor number	Factor description	Weight
F1	Familiar with Rational Unified Process	1.5
F2	Application experience	0.5
F3	Object-oriented experience	1
F4	Lead analyst capability	0.5
F5	Motivation	1
F6	Stable requirements	2
F7	Part-time workers	−1
F8	Difficult programming language	−1

Table 8-7 National Widgets Ratings

Factor number	Weight	Assigned values	Extended values	Reason
F1	1.5	1	1.5	Most of team unfamiliar
F2	0.5	1	0.5	Most of team not programmers
F3	1	1	1	Most of team not programmers
F4	0.5	5	2.5	Gus is really good
F5	1	5	5	Team is really eager
F6	2	5	10	We don't expect changes
F7	−1	0	0	No part-timers
F8	−1	2	−2	We're looking at Visual Basic

Table 8-7 shows the ratings for National Widgets. Now add all the extended values to get our EFactor:

$$1.5 + .5 + 1 + 2.5 + 5 + 10 + 0 + -2 = 18.5$$

Plugging that into our formula we get:

$$EF = 1.4 + (-0.03 * 18.5) = 0.845$$

Use Case Points

Finally, calculate use case points (UCP).

UCP = UUCP • TCF • EF

The use case points for National Widgets and the final estimation of time to complete the project is:

UCP = 80 * 0.9 * 0.845 = 60.84

Project Estimate

At this point Karner suggests using a factor of 20 man-hours per UCP for a project estimate. But a close examination of his data leads us to suggest a refinement based on our experiences with customers. Go back and look at your EF factors F1 through F8. Count how many of F1 through F6 are below 3 and how many in F7 through F8 are above 3. If the total is 2 or less, use 20 man-hours per UCP. If the total is 3 or 4, use 28 man-hours per UCP. If the total is 5 or more, try very hard to make changes to your project so the numbers can be adjusted. Your risk of failure is quite high otherwise.

Why do we suggest the changes? The EF factors concern the experience level of your staff and the stability of your project. Any negatives in this area mean you have to spend time training people or fixing problems due to instability. The more negatives you have, the more time you spend fixing problems and training people, and the less time is devoted to your project.

Because we have three negative factors, we'll multiply by 28 man-hours per UCP to get 1703.52 man-hours, which we'll round to 1704. This gives us a little under 43 weeks at 40 hours a week, or most of a year for one person.

Since we have a small team of four people, we won't run into too many problems of communication or synchronization of effort. So we'll assume they all work full-time, giving about 11 weeks of effort, and add three weeks for working out any team issues. (If you don't see why the three weeks were added onto the schedule, see Brooks, *The Mythical Man-Month*). We should have our software up and running in about 14 weeks.

CHAPTER REVIEW

By now you should have a first project plan, detailing at least the first two iterations. You also might have used the use case point estimator, or some other method, to get an idea of the man-hours needed for this project (see Table 8-8).

Table 8-8 Elaboration Phase Deliverables

Complete	Deliverables
✔	Detailed primary scenarios
✔	Secondary scenarios
✔	Activity diagrams
✔	User interface diagrammed (optional)
✔	Architecture
✔	Project plan

We suggest trying this estimator along with other project estimators you already may be using. The work was based on a small amount of research and needs to be fine tuned with more input. If you try out this estimator on your project, we really would like to hear from you. Let us know the ratings you used for the various factors and whether the results were close to the actual man-hours required to finish the project. We have even supplied a reply form in Appendix D.

The next chapter continues by giving some ideas for a review process for your documentation. It is not a formal review process, such as those required for CMM reviews, but it will give you some ideas if you don't require the formal review process.

Chapter 9

Reviews

Throughout the process of developing use cases, you will want periodic reviews of your work. These will help you find problems early. The earlier you find problems, the cheaper they are to fix, so a periodic review is worth the time it takes.

If you are already using a formal review process, continue doing so. The material in this section is not intended to be, or replace, a formal review. It is included to stimulate thought about the review process.

Many different people with many different points of view might be interested in reviewing your use cases. They may include whoever is defining your requirements, such as a customer, a marketing department, or an advisory board. End users also will be interested in the use cases when they are the actors. They also probably will want to look at your user interface description. The architect and senior technical people will want to review the use cases, architecture, risk factors, and project plan. They will be looking for completeness, clarity, and feasibility. We'll look at the various kinds of review in this chapter.

REVIEW FOR COMPLETENESS

You will want a small team, including the project architect and one or more analysts, to go through the documentation to make sure it is complete and consistent.

Gus looked up from his pile of notes. "Hey, gang, let's take a break."

"Sounds good to me!"

"Great!"

"Thought we were going to work all night!"

"Wait a minute," Gus said. "Not quite what I meant. What I meant was let's take a break from design and do a review."

"A review?! But we've been working on it steadily! Why would we need a review?"

"Well, we have been working on it steadily, and for quite a while now. What we need to do is go back and look it over again—make sure everything still makes sense and that it's consistent. Right now, we've all been concentrating on making it work. Now we need to look at it from another viewpoint and see if it makes sense. Lisa, you're a developer now. Look over what we've documented and see if it's what you need to develop the software. Dennis! You're a user . . ."

"Oh, great. Let's see, that probably means that I want to look over everything as if I know nothing about how it works, just what I can 'see' when I use it."

"That's right! Tara, you and I will look for inconsistancies. Since this is fair-sized now, it could have been infected with 'Feeping Creaturism,' and we'll want to make sure it all makes sense."

"Feeping what?" Tara burst out.

"Feeping Creaturism. That's when features creep into a project and start running away with it. Any project that goes on in time has a tendancy to gather new features. We'll go back and make sure they are actually needed and place a priority level on the ones that are."

Look at the project description, the risk factors, and the assumption list and ask yourself the following questions:

- Does the project description still make sense?
- What other influencing factors have you discovered?
- Are the risks the same as you first thought? Did any go away? Are there new ones? Have the priorities changed?
- Have any assumptions become certainties? Are there any new assumptions?

Next, look at the architecture and ask yourself:

- Do the use cases fit the architecture?
- Are all the subsystems the same? Have their descriptions changed?
- Do you need to change the interfaces either between subsystems or between the system and the outside world?

- Does the architecture account for interfaces to actors?
- Test the architecture by using the scenarios to walk through the system. Does this work? Do you have all the interfaces you need to implement the scenarios?

Review your use case diagram and use case descriptions with the following questions in mind:

- Have you found any new actors? Are some of the actors not needed?
- Have any actors moved inside the system? Has anything inside the system moved out?
- Do the names and descriptions of actors still make sense?
- Have you found any new use cases? Have you lost any?
- Do the names and descriptions of use cases still make sense?
- Do you have at least a primary scenario for each of your use cases?
- Do you have alternative and exception scenarios for all your use cases?
- Does the user interface diagram match the use cases?

All the documentation need to be updated so all parts are consistent with all the others.

REVIEW FOR POTENTIAL PROBLEMS

Now review the risk factors, market factors, and your exception scenarios. Again, you want to include the architect and one or more analysts. You are looking for the obvious problem areas in your system. For each problem discovered, determine where it can be resolved in your system. Look for groupings of problems across multiple scenarios, things that affect the system as a whole.

For example, in the order-processing system, many of the exception scenarios refer to the inventory and accounting systems being unavailable. In this case we obviously need a mechanism to hold onto requests until the systems are back online. Find ways to handle these kinds of problems in a consistent manner across the system. Add one or more modules to your architecture for the things you've added.

Resist the temptation to put in implementation details. For example, National Widgets needs an order-tracking system. Making that system a computer is an implementation detail. Instead, note that you need an order-tracking system and list its characteristics. Later you can decide the best way to handle it.

REVIEW WITH END USERS

You also will want to review the use cases and storyboards with people who will be using the system. The following are the primary questions:

- Does the system do what you expect?
- Is anything missing?
- Is there anything you don't need?
- Do you understand what the system does?
- Looking at the flows and the user interface, is the system comfortable to use?
- Does the system behave as you expect?

If user acceptance is a high risk for your project, it is important to do this review early to get acceptance from the users for your system.

REVIEW WITH CUSTOMERS

Review the list of assumptions and the use cases with whoever is defining the system, asking the following questions:

- Do you agree with the assumptions I've made?
- What needs to change?
- Do I really understand what you want?
- Is the system what you expect?
- Do you understand what the system does?

It's important to stabilize the requirements early in the process, before you have a lot invested in development. They will almost certainly change, but having stable requirements up front usually means that only minor changes will be necessary later.

REVIEW WITH DEVELOPMENT

Finally, review with the development team. Make sure everyone understands what the project is about. Keep these questions in mind:

- Does it all make sense?
- Can you build a system from the use case documents?
- What else do you need to know before you can start?

Get acceptance from your key technical people. Build their enthusiasm for this project.

REVIEWERS

Each of the review types just listed above can be more or less formal. Some groups sit around a table with copies of the documents, pizza, and cokes, and review the documents together. Other groups spend several days giving formal presentations to customers, independent verification and validation groups, and management. Then they hold follow-up meetings to discuss problems discovered and their resolution. Or you may find something in between that is useful.

What makes a good reviewer? Some people will be better at reviewing for technical content, others better at reviewing for style, consistency, and clarity. You want both kinds of reviewers. The best reviewers are those who will be honest. A review period is for finding problems. Reviewers who are too nice are not helpful. On the other hand, you don't need brutal reviewers either! Remember, all the reviewers' comments are from their point of view. Not every comment will get incorporated into the documentation. You may want some reviewers to come from outside the project. Outsiders will have an unbiased point of view and will be quick to spot areas that are unclear, inconsistent, or incomplete.

ADDING FLEXIBILITY TO YOUR SYSTEM

What if you have an overall goal that your system needs to be flexible enough to change? You might like to try the following exercise adapted from one by Stewart Brand, *How Buildings Learn*.

First, allocate one to two days for the exercise. It is best if this is offsite and the participants are undisturbed. Check your pagers and cell phones at the door, please! Then pick an exercise leader. Usually, the exercise leader is not part of the project. This person's job is to keep the exercise on track and focused on the issues. This is a good job for a skilled outside consultant.

The exercise leader spends a week or so before the exercise interviewing the major players in the project. This may include the project sponsor, senior management, the lead architect, or the senior technical staff. The exercise leader interviews these people to find out what they consider the major issues ("What keeps you awake at night?") and what their expectations are about the future of the system under development. The exercise leader also becomes familiar with the vocabulary of the project. What are the buzzwords and common expressions in use around the project?

Then the project sponsor, project manager, chief architect, and lead technical people gather for a one-to-two day session. Unless the project is huge, this should be five or fewer people from the project plus the exercise leader. This is not an exercise for the whole project team. If your team has only five people, the project sponsor and the project manager will join the exercise leader. If the project manager is not also the lead technical person, you will add that person to the group as well. The group will need the exercise leader's interview notes, plus the project documentation that has been written to date.

The first day begins with identifying the need for the project. ("Why are you building this system?") This is not the same as the project description. The project description defines what you are building. This part of the exercise is exploring why you are building it.

Then the group explores the market forces that could affect this project. These will include things such as changes in technology, regulation by various government agencies, what the competition is doing, customer demands, and changes in the customer base. The group ranks these market forces in terms of importance and uncertainty. The most important and most uncertain are at the top of the list. The important uncertainties could cause the failure of the project. The group also makes a list of what they consider to be reliable certainties for their project, such as new and faster systems coming out at least once a year.

Next, the group identifies and spells out the "official future" of the system, the one that everyone thinks they are supposed to expect. ("We'll never have more than 5,000 users at a time.") The exercise leader has interview material as a starting point. Then, the group takes the official future and modifies it using the list of important uncertainties. Each modification gives another possible future. The group will end up with a whole set of possible futures for your system.

In the next step, the group must start thinking the unthinkable. Let people top each other in imagining terrible and delightful things that might happen to your system. ("Every baby boomer in the world signs up for an online account at once.") Use these to modify the official future. Add these new modifications to your set of possible futures. The goal is to find new, plausible futures that are surprising or even shocking.

Sleep on that. The next day the group revisits the futures, adjusts them, names them, and picks two to five of the most plausible. Using memorable names for the futures helps people remember them and differentiate between them. Of the two to five plausible futures, don't worry about which one is most likely to occur. Do include at least one wildcard future that is considered unlikely but horrifying if it were to occur. Write detailed, vivid stories for the futures to bring them to life and make them real.

Take the two to five plausible futures and storylines, and compare them to your project description, use case diagram, architecture diagram, and use case descriptions. What has to change to allow any of the two to five new futures to be handled, if they were to occur? Is it possible for the system to be made flexible enough to accommodate all the new possibilities? Look at the project scope and the project plan. Can these changes be incorporated in the time frame and budget we have allowed?

Go back to the project risk analysis. What new risks have you discovered? Do some regret analysis. Ask, "What if we get it wrong? What would we regret not having done? What would we regret locking in?"

Make decisions on what to keep in the project and what to change based on the exercise. Update all the documentation to reflect these decisions. Go back and share the results with the project team.

CHAPTER REVIEW

In this chapter we considered various ways of looking at a project, including technically, user focused, market demand, and the needs of the future. Although we only talk about reviews in this chapter, they are something that should be applied during every phase of the project. By now you should understand your system very well and be ready to build it. The next chapter looks at the role of use cases in constructing and delivering a system.

Chapter 10

Constructing and Delivering a System

We have spent a lot of time learning about our system and what we want it to do. Now we need to move forward and decide how we are going to construct the system. We'll start by identifying the key abstractions in the system. Then we'll show how the key abstractions relate to the use cases, architecture, and project plan. The rest of our construction activities center around an iteration. We look at planning, testing, and reviewing the iteration, using the documents we have previously written. Finally, we consider the uses of use cases when preparing the product for market and beyond.

KEY ABSTRACTIONS OF THE DOMAIN

We'll start by identifying the key abstractions of the system. Key abstractions are things that are important and meaningful in your system. They are the primary things you work with in creating your system. They are the words you use to describe your domain.

The domain is the subject area you are working in. Some examples of domains are mail order companies, satellite communications, voice messaging, accounting, machine controllers, hospital administration, and library management. Obviously, this list is not exhaustive! Within a domain, your project is solving a particular problem. Both the domain and the problem have a vocabulary you use to describe them. That vocabulary expresses the key abstractions of your system.

"Okay, Gus. How do we go from use cases to software?"

"We need to find key abstractions and detail what they mean."

"What's a key abstraction?"

"Key abstractions are the things we use in our order-processing system."

"Would that be like a computer? Or Gus?" Lisa asked.

"No!" Gus laughed. "No, nothing like that. It would be like our products and the order forms we fill out. Those would be key abstractions."

"So a key abstraction is something that gets used or manipulated in our use cases? Okay, I can understand that. So, how do we find them?"

Identifying Key Abstractions in Use Cases

Some of the key abstractions will be obvious; these are the things you use in creating a system in a particular domain. For example, in an order-processing system, we know we are going to be dealing with orders. Others won't be as obvious. Ivar Jacobson described a way to think about your system that helps identify the key abstractions. He defined three kinds of abstractions—entity, boundary, and controller. These have been included as kinds of classes in the UML.

An entity is something that is saved, updated, and manipulated. It represents the data elements in your system. Entities are usually passive things without much behavior. They are frequently found as parameters to function calls and are stored in databases. Look for things that you store and retrieve. These will become entity classes.

A boundary is something that represents an interface between the system and its actors. The boundary can be a screen on a user interface or the calls you make to another system. A boundary class is responsible for knowing how to interact with an actor. Look at your use case diagrams. When an actor communicates with the system, you need a boundary class to handle that communication. Define a boundary class that displays a screen and handles user input. Another boundary class can be defined to send messages to and receive messages from another system.

A *controller* is something that knows the logic of the system and manages some activity. A controller also can be something that controls access to some shared resource. This could be hardware, such as a printer, or software, such as an error log or a database. A controller usually is active, interacting with the boundaries and using the entities. Look for things that are shared in your system and activities that need managing. Define controller classes to manage them.

"First,"Gus started, "let's look for things we store and retrieve."

"You mean the stuff we want in the database?" Dennis asked.

"Right."

"Okay, then that's . . . order, product and customer."

"Wait," Lisa added, "isn't customer part of order?"

"Maybe, but we won't know for sure until we try working with it. So we'll leave customer in for now."

"What about accounts?" asked Tara, as she looked through the use cases.

"We never directly deal with accounts. The accounting system does, so we don't have to worry about them."

"Well then, products are the same!"

"No, we actually do quite a bit with products."

"Sigh. All right, is that everything then?"

"Well, no," Gus laughed. "Now we need things to represent the boundaries."

"Boundaries?" Dennis asked. "Boundaries to what?"

"Between our system and the actors."

"Oh, like that rectangle on our use case diagram!" Tara laughed.

"Sure! What things know about that boundary?"

"You mean, like the screens?" Lisa said, "They know about it?"

"Right. They know about the boundary because they are in our system and deal with actors outside our system. What other boundaries do we have?"

"To the inventory system."

"The accounting system."

"What about interfaces to subsystems?"

"No, they're inside the system."

"But we can treat each subsystem as a system! Gus said so!" Tara said.

"She's right," Gus interjected.

"Well then," Dennis said, "do the subsystems have entities?"

"They certainly use them."

"Any we've missed so far?" Gus asked, looking up from his notes.

"Yes! Access permission! Or rather, login information in general."

"Pick lists and mailing labels."

"Mailing label is just customer printed out. Good thing we made it a separate entity."

"Let me catch up a second" Gus muttered, as he wrote. "Okay, then. We'll keep the others. Now we need controllers. They manage resources and activities in the system."

"The database. It's a resource, right? So we need a database manager."

Tara objected with, "Won't the interface do it?"

"No. The interface just passes on requests from the actors into the sub-system," Dennis said. "A database manager to control those requests is a great idea!"

"Okay, then. Inventory and accounting."

"I think they manage themselves, but we should find out," said Gus. "For now, we'll assume they have controllers of their own. Add that to the list of assumptions, Tara! Now, let's fill these out with brief descriptions."

Key Abstractions for Order Processing

Order—at a minimum, a list of products with prices, a shipping address, and payment information

Product—information about products including at a minimum, the product code, a description, the price, and the stock on hand in the warehouse

Customer—information about a customer including at a minimum, their name and address

Screen—the user interface

Subsystem boundary—an interface to a subsystem

User login info—at a minimum, user name, password, and access restrictions

Pick list—a list of products and quantities

Database manager—something that controls access to the database

Diagramming Scenarios with Key Abstractions

Now that you have found some key abstractions, you can use them in sequence diagrams to represent the significant scenarios of a use case. A sequence diagram is used to show abstractions in your system and the messages passed between them. It is time ordered from top to bottom. The UML has a very rich notation for sequence diagrams. We will use a small part of it for these first sequence diagrams.

Select a use case and start with its primary scenario. Identify the key abstractions used in the primary scenario. Put them across the top of a page with a vertical line under each to represent time. Also on the top of the page, draw stick figures to represent the actors that participate in the scenario.

Now go through the scenario looking for behavior. Draw horizontal bars between the vertical lines to show behavior happening between actors and key abstractions, and any information that goes with the behavior. Clear as mud, right? Let's do an example.

We'll do a sequence diagram for the primary scenario of the Find Order use case from the Manage Orders subsystem, taking the branch in which the user enters an order ID and assume we were canceling an order. The three key abstractions we'll use to implement this use case are the Order, Find Order, and Cancel Order screens. The actors for this use case are customer and database, which we'll represent with stick figures. The other abstractions go in boxes.

Find Order Use Case

1. The use case starts when a Find Order request is received.
2. The system displays the Find Order screen.
3. The user enters an order ID.
4. The user selects Search.
5. The system asks the database for an order record.
6. The system returns an order and the use case ends.

In Exhibit 10-1, the user tells Cancel Order to find an order. Then Cancel Order creates the Find Order screen with the command Display. Then the user enters an order ID and presses Search. The Find Order screen sends a request to the database to get an order based on the order ID. The database returns that order to the Find Order screen. That's the end of this use case.

Exhibit 10-1 Find Order Sequence Diagram

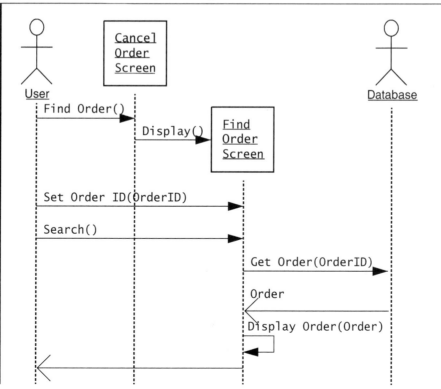

As you create the sequence diagrams, you may find that you need new things in your system. For example, during Place Order we send credit information to the accounting system to charge the account. That information is part of the order, but because it also needs to be passed to the accounting system, we might decide to make it into an abstraction of its own.

Diagramming Key Abstractions

The sequence diagrams helped us find which abstractions we needed to implement each use case. We also found messages the abstractions had to respond to. We'll capture that information in a class diagram for each use case. We call this class diagram a view of participating classes for the use case. In the UML, we say this is a collaboration that realizes the use case.

We will use classes to represent the key abstractions. In the UML, a class is represented by a rectangle. Draw a rectangle for each key abstraction and divide it into three compartments. The first holds the name of the abstraction. The second describes data it uses. The third describes messages it receives. For each use case, create a diagram showing the classes needed by that use case, as shown in Exhibit 10-2.

We got the information about the Find Order and Cancel Order screens from the sequence diagram. We know what data Order needs to hold from its description when we identified it. We don't currently know of any behavior for Order. We don't show the user or the database because they are actors, not part of our system. Exhibit 10-2 shows the parts of the system that implement Find Order.

In the project plan, we identified use cases to develop for each iteration. The view of participating classes for those use cases tells us which classes to develop for the iteration. The same class can appear on more than one view of participating classes. That simply means that part of the class will be used to implement one use case, and part of the class will be used to implement another use case.

Exhibit 10-2 View of Participating Classes for Find Order Use Case

Find Order Screen	Order	Cancel Order Screen

`OrderID`	`OrderID`
	`CustomerInfo`
	`ListofProducts`
	`PaymentInfo`	

`Display()`
`SetOrderedID()`
`Search()`
		`FindOrder()`

Exhibit 10-3 Product Information Subsystem

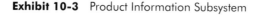

Product Information Boundary
GetProductInfo(Product code) UpdateProductQuantities(Product, Quantity) MarkProductBack-ordered(Product, Quantity) Back-orderedItemsArrived()

Product
ProductCode Description Price StockonHand

Manage Back-orders
MarkProductBack-ordered(Product, Quantity) Back-orderedItemsArrived()

In addition to creating class diagrams for use cases, we also will create one class diagram for each subsystem. This class diagram will contain the classes we need to implement the behavior identified for the subsystem. In the UML, we say this is a collaboration that realizes the subsystem. You can find the behavior by looking at the use case diagram for the subsystem, and by looking at the subsystem operations. A diagram for the product information subsystem is shown in Exhibit 10-3.

Because we decided to create a boundary class to handle the interface to the product information subsystem, we put the subsystem operations into that class.

Classes inside a subsystem usually have a lot in common. Putting them together on a class diagram helps you find similarities between classes. Taking advantage of the similarities makes coding easier.

Use Case versus Architectural View

We end up with two very different views of our system. The use case view shows the work flows throughout the system and helps us maintain consistency throughout that work flow. It is a good basis for black box testing and user guides because it shows the outside view of the system. The architectural view shows the subsystems that make up the system and helps us maintain consistency within the subsystems. The subsystems are the basis of reuse and maintenance in your system. These are things you can buy if you decide not to build all of your system yourself.

Exhibit 10-4 Classes and Scenarios

	ProductInfo::Product	Database::DatabaseBoundary	ProductInfo::ProductInfoBoundary	ManageOrders::Order	MoneyHandling::MoneyHandlingBoundary	OrderDept::CustomerInfo	ShipOrders::ShipOrdersBoundary
Back-ordered items received	X	X	X	X			

You may find it helpful to create a chart like the one in Exhibit 10-4, showing how use cases relate to subsystems through classes. First, list use cases down one side; then list classes across the top using this naming convention:

```
subsystem::class name
```

Put an X in the box if the use case uses that class.

This helps make it clear that a use case describes a workflow through some of the classes in the architecture. Reading across the row, we see the classes that make up the use cases. Down the column we see which use cases the class participates in.

THE ITERATION SCHEDULE

You are ready to start the first iteration. Looking at the project plan, you know how long you have to build it, what you are going to build, and how you are going to test it. Spend a little time at the beginning of the iteration reviewing this information with your team. Determine dependencies in the software and make sure that software that is used by most of the team is developed first.

Set aside some time at the end of the iteration to review the iteration, update documentation, and firm up plans for the next two iterations. Imagine that the first iteration is scheduled for September 1 through September 22.

- Sept. 1—spend the day planning the work assignments
- Sept. 2 through Sept. 21—code the first set of use cases
    - `OrderProduct`, primary scenario only
    - `GiveProductInfo`, primary scenario only
    - `UpdateAccount`, primary scenario only
    - `GetStatusOnOrder`, primary scenario only
- Sept. 22—review and plan the next set of activities

The coding part of the iteration will include analysis, design, coding, and testing. See Appendix A for books about software development and testing.

Because use cases describe the behavior of the system, we can use them to test the code. Does the software act and react as described in the use cases? If not, why?

At the end of the iteration, take some time to review and update all project documentation.

- Look at what you actually accomplished and compare it to the goals for this iteration. Did you meet your goals? Why or why not? If there are some use cases that did not get built, where will they go in the project plan?
- What have you learned about risk factors? Do changes need to made to your list of risks? If so, how does that effect your project plan?
- Look at your use cases. Have any changed? Have any gone away? Have you added new use cases? Where do they fit into your project plan?
- Look at the actors. Have any changed or gone away? Did you add new actors? What happens to the use cases associated with these actors?
- What changes have you made to your architecture?

Go back and update your project documents to reflect any changes you need to make because of what you learned. Update your project plan as needed. Focus especially on the next two iterations.

You also may need to schedule a project review with management, marketing, sales teams, or end users. Use your updated project documents to pull together a presentation. Is there something you can demo in your current system? You might be able to demo by creating a quick command line interface to your code, if the user interface does not yet exist.

DELIVERY AND BEYOND

This phase of project development is where you turn your system into a product. Some of the things that get created in the transition phase are:

- User guides
- Training materials
- Sales kits
- Demos
- Marketing plans
- Ad campaigns

The documentation you have been creating, particularly use cases, will help you develop these various documents during the transition phase.

As the project progresses, you must keep the documents up to date. Many people are depending on the information to be correct. The ultimate success of the project depends on all the parts working together—the system with its validated testing, user manuals, training, and sales kits.

You won't want to share all the documentation, but only the parts that represent what you are actually delivering. You may have use cases for everything you will eventually do with a product, but the first version being delivered to customers may implement only a subset of those use cases. The rest will come in a later release. You won't want user guides or training covering features that don't exist yet. You also don't want sales or marketing to tell customers about features that the product won't have.

User Guides and Training

Technical writers will want the descriptions of use cases and their scenarios as a starting point for user guides. Each use case with its alternatives and exceptions describes to the user how the system behaves and how they interact with it. The use cases can be put together with screen shots of the user interface as a starting point for a user guide.

This first cut at a user guide also could be a starting point for training materials for end users. You will want to put the material into slide format and create exercises, but the basic information you need to use the system is in the use cases.

Sales Kits and Marketing Literature

Use cases can provide the basis for the "What our product does" part of the sales kits and marketing material. Looking through the use cases, marketing people can find the features you are building. Be sure marketing knows what you are really delivering. The use cases you share may be a subset of all the possible use cases.

The project plan also will be of interest to marketing. With information on what features will be finished when, they can design alpha and beta release programs, as well as develop product announcements and plan advertising campaigns.

Marketing or the engineering team may want to put together demos of the product. The steps of the use cases can be put together to create a script showing the functionality of the system.

Use Cases after Delivery

The use cases you have written contain a lot of information about your domain as well as the system you have actually built. This information is historical but also can be used as a starting point for creating a repository of information for developing a line of business.

The next project you construct in the same domain will have many similarities to the current project. The new team can look over the existing use cases and modify them for the new system. This is a lot faster than developing all this information new each time a project is started.

The use cases are also a repository of knowledge that can be shared with new employees. In most cases, when someone is hired for a project, they get information about the project from the other people working on it. Having a set of use cases to review gives the new person a lot of information without taking time from other team members. This knowledge store also is available when key people leave the project or the company. The people are no longer available, but what they knew about the project is captured in the use cases and their associated information.

CHAPTER REVIEW

In this chapter, we have looked at numerous possible uses of use cases in construction, delivery, and beyond. There are a lot of good books about software development and software testing. For more information on these topics, interested readers should refer to Appendix A. Things you may have created during this phase of development include those shown in Table 10-1 on the next page.

Table 10-1 Construction Phase Deliverables

Complete	Deliverables
✔	Iteration plans
✔	Code
✔	Test plans
✔	Test results
✔	Review of iteration
✔	User guides
✔	Training manuals
✔	Demos
✔	Sales and marketing materials

FINAL WRAP-UP

We can't promise that if you follow the steps, your software will be wonderful. We do believe that you will understand your project better, which is the first step toward building better systems. You will spend a lot of time on analysis—probably 25 percent of the total project schedule. But this time is made up later during construction because the projects' problems were addressed at the beginning. Working with use cases tends to bring out project issues early. Better to deal with them in analysis than while everyone is busy coding.

Like any project, this book had deadlines to meet. Although we would like to say the book is perfect in every way, we must admit that we are continuing to work on the material. The UML is currently going through a review process, and we expect some of that work to affect this book. Where can you get the most up-to-date information? Visit our Web site at *http://books.txt.com* or e-mail us at *books@txt.com*.

Appendix A

Resource List

This appendix includes short list of some books we have found interesting and thought provoking over the years. We've included books about OOAD, project management, patterns and idioms, architecture, sociology, and market trends. We like to look at software projects from a variety of perspectives, so some of these books are not software books, specifically; they are books that stimulated thought and gave us new perspectives on software development.

Bellin, D., Simone, S. 1997. *The CRC Card Book.* Reading, MA: Addison Wesley Longman.

> CRC cards are a great team approach to determining the responsibilities of classes and their collaborations with other classes. They are especially nice for groups new to OO.

Booch, G. 1996. *Best of Booch.* New York: SIGS Books.

> A collection of essays by Grady on everything to do with software development.

Booch, G. 1994. *Object-Oriented Analysis and Design With Application.* Reading, MA: Addison Wesley Longman.

> A really good book on object-oriented analysis and design. Look for the 3rd edition in 1999, which will be UML-based.

Booch, G. 1996. *Object Solutions.* Reading, MA: Addison Wesley Longman.

> A great explanation of managing your software project.

Brand, S. 1994. *How Buildings Learn.* New York: Penguin Books.

> An interesting book on the architecture of buildings. But check out Chapter 11, The Scenario-Buffered Building. Lots of good stuff in there that can apply to software.

Brooks, F. 1995. *The Mythical Man-Month: Anniversary Edition.* Reading, MA: Addison Wesley Longman.

> A classic must-read.

Buschmann, F., R. Meunier, H. Rohnert, P. Sommerlad, and M. Stal. 1996. *Pattern-Oriented Software Architecture: A System of Patterns.* West Sussex, England: Wiley.

A good book on software architecture patterns and design patterns extending the work of Gamma, et al.

Fowler, M. 1997. *Analysis Patterns.* Reading, MA: Addison Wesley Longman.

Patterns applied to problems at the analysis stage of software development.

Fowler, M. with K. Scott. 1997. *UML Distilled: Applying the Standard Object Modeling Language.* Menlo Park, CA: Addison-Wesley.

With all the UML books out, this is still the best overview of the core parts of the UML, the parts everyone can use.

Gamma, E., R. Helm, R. Johnson, and J. Vlissides. 1995. *Design Patterns: Elements of Object-Oriented Architecture.* Reading, MA: Addison Wesley Longman.

THE book on design patterns. Describes well-known design problems and gives patterns of solutions. Everyone refers to this as the GOF (Gang of Four) book.

Hohmann, L. 1997. *Journey of the Software Professional: A Sociology of Software Development.* Upper Saddle River, NJ: Prentice-Hall.

The care and feeding of your development team. A must-read for managers, with a bunch of great parts for programmers as well. How do engineers think? How to create teams that can work together? What kind of environment do engineers need to be most effective on the job?

Jacobson, I., M. Christerson, P. Jonsson, and G. Oevergaard. 1992. *Object-Oriented Software Engineering.* New York: ACM Press.

The original use case book. Jacobson's methodology has been largely incorporated into the UML. This is an alternate viewpoint to software development from Booch and Rumbaugh. Combined in the UML, these methodologies help you develop a more well-rounded application.

Jacobson, I., M. Ericsson, and A. Jacobson. 1995. *The Object Advantage.* New York: ACM Press.

Applies OO techniques and use cases to business processes.

Popcorn, F., and L. Marigold. 1996. *Clicking.* New York: HarperCollins.
Popcorn, F. 1992. *The Popcorn Report.* New York: HarperCollins.

These two books are on market trends in society. These might be useful to look at for ideas when doing risk analysis for your product.

Rumbaugh, J., M. Blaha, W. Premerlani, F. Eddy, and W. Lorensen. 1991. *Object-Oriented Modeling and Design.* Englewood Cliffs, NJ: Prentice-Hall.

Another classic OOAD book. The notation is quite similar to UML.

Rumbaugh, J. 1996. *OMT Insights.* New York: SIGS Books.

A collection of articles on software development.

Shaw, M. and D. Garlan 1996. *Software Architecture: Perspectives on an Emerging Discipline.* Englewood Cliffs, NJ: Prentice-Hall.

A well-written book on software architecture patterns. Great for ideas when developing your own architectures.

Taylor, D. 1998. *Object-Oriented Technology: A Manager's Guide, Second Edition.* Reading, MA: Addison Wesley Longman.

> Need an easy book on OO terminology for your boss? This is it. No one has done it better.

Webster, B. 1995. *Pitfalls of Object Oriented Development.* New York: M & T Books.

> We all know that sometimes things go a bit wrong on a project. This book lists a number of pitfalls, tells how you can detect when you are in trouble, and what to do to correct the situation.

Here are a couple of our favorite books for those times when you need to rest the conscious brain and let the subconscious work on the problem.

Anthony, Piers. Any of the *Xanth* books—there are about 20 of them. Published by Del Ray, New York; Avon, New York; and Tor, New York.

> Definitely light reading, but if you like puns, you'll love these books.

Eddings, David. *The Belgariad and the Mallorean series*, about 12 rather thick books. Published by Del Ray, New York.

> Good guys, bad guys, and fair maidens to be won. But the characters are deep, fully formed, and interesting.

McKinley, Robin. 1978. *Beauty.* New York: Pocket Books.

> The BEST telling of the story Beauty and the Beast, ever. You might cry. It's okay.

Appendix B

Documentation Templates

These templates have been written up for Frame, Word, and as text files. They can be found at *http://books.txt.com*

SYSTEM OR SUBSYSTEM DOCUMENTS

System Name

<Brief description. In a large system, this could be several pages. Note this is not meant to be detailed requirements, but a basic overview of the system.>

Risk Factors

<List risk factors here in priority order.>

System-Level Use Case Diagram

<Or you could just list the actors and use cases in text.>

Architecture Diagram

<Include a description of the interfaces as well. These could be on the diagram or listed in text.>

Subsystem Descriptions

<Include a brief description of each subsystem.>

USE CASE DOCUMENT

Use Case Name

<Brief description. Usually a paragraph or less.>

Actors

<A list of the actors who communicate with this use case.>

Priority

<How important is this use case to the project?>

Status

<What point are we in developing this use case?>

Preconditions

<A list of conditions that must be true before the use case starts.>

Postconditions

<A list of conditions that must be true when the use case ends, no matter which scenario is executed.>

Extension Points

<If the use case has extension points, list them here.>

"Used" Use Cases

<If the use case uses other use cases, list them here.>

Flow of Events

<This could be a basic path and alternative paths, or the primary scenario.>

Activity Diagram

<An activity diagram of the flow of events, or some significant or complex part of the flow of events.>

User Interface

<For systems that interface with people, include a description of the user interface, possibly using storyboards.>

Secondary Scenarios

<If alternatives and exceptions are not shown in the flow of events, scenarios should be listed here and may include a brief description.>

Sequence Diagrams

<If you don't have separate documents for scenarios, you might include sequence diagrams for them here.>

Subordinate Use Cases

<If the use case has subordinate use cases, show them here. Or you could include a use case diagram for the subordinate use cases. Or both. Also tell what subsystem is responsible for this subordinate use case.>

View of Participating Classes

<A collaboration showing all the classes whose objects interact to implement this use case. You also can show interfaces to the use case here and which of the classes implement the interfaces.>

Other Artifacts

<This can include references to the subsystem the use case belongs to, an analysis model, a design model, code, or test plans.>

Other Requirements

<This section is where you can put nonfunctional requirements affecting the use case.>

SCENARIO DOCUMENT

Scenario Name

<Brief description—usually a paragraph or less.>

Use Case

<The use case this scenario is part of.>

Priority

<How important is this scenario to the project?>

Status

<What point are we in developing this scenario?>

Flow of Events

<This could be a basic path and alternative paths, or the primary scenario.

Activity Diagram

<An activity diagram of the flow of events, or some significant or complex part of the flow of events.>

Sequence Diagrams

<A sequence diagram of the flow of events of the scenario.>

Other Artifacts

<This can include references to an analysis model, a design model, code, or test plans.>

Appendix C

UML Notation Used in This Book

This Appendix only contains a subset of the UML notation. It is not intended to teach the notation, but to provide a quick reference to the parts of the UML we used in the book.

Exhibit C-1   Use Case Diagram Notation

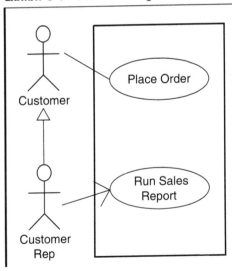

Actors are Customer and Customer Rep. Use cases are Place Order and Run Sales Report.

Customer Rep inherits from Customer, so Customer Rep may use Place Order as well as Run Sales Report. Customer may use only Place Order.

The communicates relationship is between actor and use case. The arrow shows who starts the use case. Customer Rep starts Run Sales Report. We don't know who starts Place Order.

The rectangle around the use cases marks the system boundary.

Exhibit C-1 Use Case Diagram Notation (*Continued*)

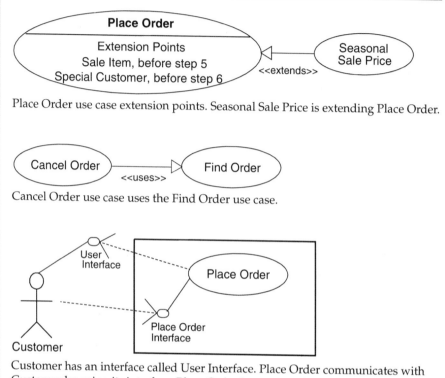

Place Order use case extension points. Seasonal Sale Price is extending Place Order.

Cancel Order use case uses the Find Order use case.

Customer has an interface called User Interface. Place Order communicates with Customer by using its interface. Place Order has an interface called Place Order Interface. Customer communicates with Place Order by using its interface.

Exhibit C-2 Packages Notation

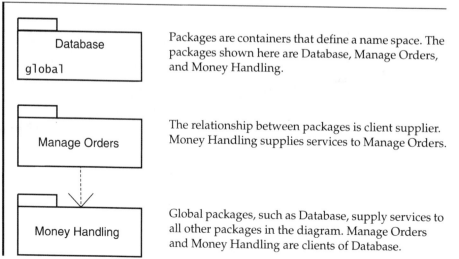

Packages are containers that define a name space. The packages shown here are Database, Manage Orders, and Money Handling.

The relationship between packages is client supplier. Money Handling supplies services to Manage Orders.

Global packages, such as Database, supply services to all other packages in the diagram. Manage Orders and Money Handling are clients of Database.

Exhibit C-3 Activity Diagram Notation

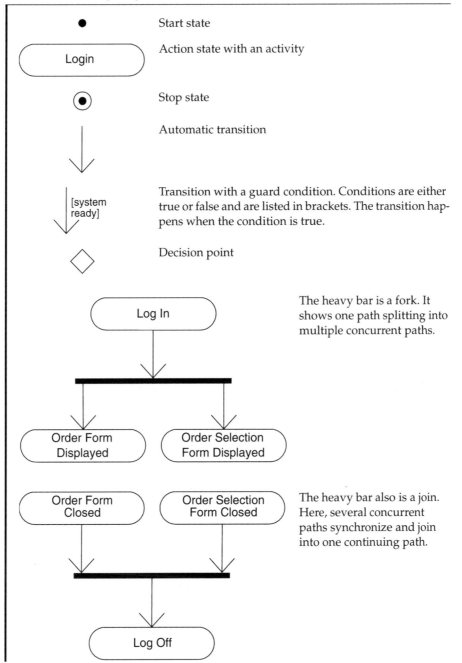

Start state

Action state with an activity

Stop state

Automatic transition

Transition with a guard condition. Conditions are either true or false and are listed in brackets. The transition happens when the condition is true.

Decision point

The heavy bar is a fork. It shows one path splitting into multiple concurrent paths.

The heavy bar also is a join. Here, several concurrent paths synchronize and join into one continuing path.

Exhibit C-4 Sequence Diagram Notation

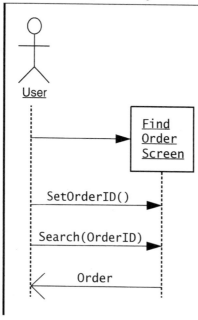

Objects are rectangles containing an underlined name. We also include instances of actors. Because they are instances, the names are underlined.

The dotted vertical line is the object lifeline, showing when it exists. A message into the side of the object means it is being created.

The solid arrows are synchronous messages or procedure calls. The stick arrow is a return.

Exhibit C-5 Class Diagram Notation

Find Order Screen
OrderID
Display() SetOrderedID() Search()

A class is a rectangle with three compartments. The first contains the name of the class, the second the attributes of the class, and the third the operations of the class.

Database

Database Facade
SaveOrder(Order) UpdateOrderStatus()

We also show a package containing a class. If the contents of a package are simple, you may choose to show them directly in the package, as we have done here. Note the name of the package has moved into the tab.

Appendix D

Reply Form for the Use Case Estimator

We are interested in continuing the work on estimating projects with use cases. If you try the use case estimator, we would be interested in hearing from you. Did it give you accurate results? Would you modify it? How and why?

In addition we would like to have a brief description of your project. We're looking here for something like—It was a small distributed business application. The project team was five people, two of whom were expert in object orientation, with the rest new to it. The code was written in Visual Basic and used CORBA, which the whole team knew quite well.

If you are able to include your project description, we would be interested in seeing that as well.

Did you change any of the weights? Which ones and why?

Did you find the factors useful? Did you add or delete any factors? Which ones and why?

You can send us the information via e-mail at *books@txt.com*

For your information, we have reproduced the technical and environmental factors tables here.

Table D-1 Technical Factors for System and Weights

Factor number	Factor description	Weight
T1	Distributed system	2
T2	Response or throughput performance objectives	1
T3	End user efficiency (on-line)	1
T4	Complex internal processing	1
T5	Code must be reusable	1
T6	Easy to install	0.5
T7	Easy to use	0.5
T8	Portable	2
T9	Easy to change	1
T10	Concurrent	1
T11	Includes special security features	1
T12	Provides direct access for third parties	1
T13	Special user training facilities are required	1

Table D-2 Environmental Factors for Team and Weights

Factor number	Factor description	Weight
F1	Familiar with Rational Unified Process	1.5
F2	Application experience	0.5
F3	Object-oriented experience	1
F4	Lead analyst capability	0.5
F5	Motivation	1
F6	Stable requirements	2
F7	Part-time workers	−1
F8	Difficult programming language	−1

Index